An impassioned sense of urgency runs through Kirk Schneider's *The Vibrant Center: A New Consciousness for Our Broken Age.* It is "a call to awareness" targeted at parenting, education, work and employment, religion, government, politics, and, ultimately, all of our world relations in order that we reconnect with the fundamentally human commitment to co-create a better world not only for ourselves but for all humankind. Always challenging, at times discomforting in its honesty, this is a deeply relevant book full of concrete wisdom, humor, and inspirational commitment. Always accessible, packed with insightful and revealing reflections from Dr. Schneider's own life as well as from the lives of other notable individuals, *The Vibrant Center* reminds us of the realistic possibilities available when we open ourselves to the possibilities and responsibilities of existence. No doubt about it: This is a book for our times.

Professor Ernesto Spinelli, author of *Practising Existential Therapy: The Relational World.*

We are living through a moment of dangerous either/or thinking—in our politics, our institutions, our most intimate relationships. Kirk Schneider's powerful alternative—*The Vibrant Center*—takes us to a new consciousness and asks how we can embed that integrative approach in our lives, our relationships, and our societies. This book shows, concretely and convincingly, what it looks like to parent, teach, lead, and govern from that place of deeper connection. It is one of the most important calls to awareness I have encountered in years.

Wendy Smith, Author of *Both/And Thinking: Embracing Creative Tensions to Solve Your Toughest Problems*

I love the whole concept of this book and I'm so glad Kirk Schneider wrote it. It's a much-needed book for our times.

Scott Barry Kaufman, author of *Transcend: The New Science of Self-Actualization*

The Vibrant Center is a personal and wide-ranging book that challenges us to think about psychological depth beyond the clinic as a civic and cultural matter. The book brings together existential-humanistic thought and practical proposals for reforming aspects of our lives from parenting to governance. Schneider insists on the necessity of the difficult, ongoing work of holding complexity. The underlying vision of a society that takes inner life seriously as a foundation for collective well-being continues to deserve sustained attention and debate.

Awais Aftab, MD, Clinical Associate Professor of Psychiatry, Case Western Reserve University; Editor, *Conversations in Critical Psychiatry* (Oxford University Press, 2024)

For over a decade, I have been deeply drawn to Dr. Schneider's ideas on existential-depth psychology; he is a constant innovator. From "awe" to the "fluid center," and currently to the "vibrant center," he has synthesized his past existential thought and taken it to new heights. Dr. Schneider has always focused his concern on the human condition, and his greatest contribution to human well-being lies in his ongoing endeavor to provide or awaken that vibrant center in human life—which, in a more specific way, realizes what Rollo May referred to as the "center of strength."

Xuefu Wang, Founder of the Zhi-Mian Institute for Psychotherapy, Nanjing, China

The Vibrant Center is a bold attempt to grapple with the galloping polarization, dehumanization, and alienation we face in the 21st century. It alerts us to the tremendous dangers we face if we do not attempt to remedy them in all spheres of our lives: politics, education, parenting, spirituality, and work. Schneider's reflections on "resilient luminaries," or the courageous thinkers, artists, and activists who embodied the traits we are so deeply in danger of losing—Viktor Frankl, Simone de Beauvoir, Nelson Mandela, Stephen Hawking, Federico Garcia Lorca, Maya Angelou and others—remind us that even in the face of adversity, we can rise above the barriers that prevent us from experiencing, embodying, and promoting the most precious and redeeming human qualities in our own lives.

Daniel Burston, Professor Emeritus and former Chair of Psychology at Duquesne University, author of *The Wing of Madness: The Life and Work of R.D. Laing*

Refreshingly honest and abundant with ideas, the moral courage of this book is exhibited both by its unconventional diagnosis of humanity's current state and its call for sweeping social changes. Our lives have been broken—fractured by extremism, dogma, and divisive ideology. *The Vibrant Center* poses audacious questions about healing, possibilities, and what a true democratic republic demands of us. What could be more important now than the collective endeavor to build vibrant worlds and lives worth living?

Zenobia Morrill, PhD, Assistant Professor of Clinical Psychology, William James College

This book is both erudite and pragmatic. In *The Vibrant Center*, Kirk Schneider draws on some of the best thinkers of modern times to propose a framework for how ethically and morally to use our authority to move forward as human beings. From politics to parenting to religion, he provides a roadmap for how we humans can behave better, and he believes we have it in us to do so.

Maureen O'Reilly-Landry, PhD, Teaching Faculty, NYU Postdoctoral Program in Psychotherapy & Psychoanalysis

I found *The Vibrant Center* to be innovative, refreshing, idealistic-aspirational, and very relevant to the dangerously polarized times that we are living in. Although Schneider's far-reaching descriptions of what he refers to as the "vibrant center" may appear unrealistic to achieve on a societal level, he has admirably given us descriptions of how he has been putting his ideas into practice. Schneider describes his vibrant center thesis in a number of realms—such as parenting, education, the workforce, and government—but, personally, I found his political depolarization and dialogue descriptions particularly relevant. Also, Schneider made the educated guess that the influential political organization *Indivisible* would welcome his ideas about the vibrant center, and as an active member of *Indivisible*, I wholeheartedly agree with Schneider. In particular, *Indivisible* strongly advocates for direct actions involving protests and demonstrations, but it also recommends dialogue with one's Members of Congress in their repertoire of activities to save democracy in the United States. I have used both of these *Indivisible* actions, and they are very consistent with Schneider's both/and approach as well as the central thesis of his vibrant center ideas.

Elliot Benjamin, Active member of *Indivisible*, Bangor, Maine, and author of *The Creative Artist, Mental Disturbance, and Mental Health*

The Vibrant Center: A New Consciousness for Our Broken Age is an "invitation" to participate both interpersonally and intrapersonally with the cultivation of presence. Kirk Schneider's heartfelt vision and appeal to what Kierkegaard termed the "Solitary Individual" (or person who lives presently and responsibly) is invaluable for leading our species into a sensibility that promotes civility and quality of life.

Jim Hernandez, Depth Healer, Founder and Director of The Center for Inner Peace; formerly Youth Violence Prevention Specialist, Concord Police Department, Concord, CA

The Vibrant Center
A New Consciousness for Our Broken Age

By Kirk Schneider, PhD

Colorado Springs, CO
www.universityprofessorspress.com

The Vibrant Center: A New Consciousness for Our Broken Age
By Kirk J. Schneider

ISBN (Hardcover): 978-1-955737-74-6
ISBN (Paperback): 978-1-955737-75-3
ISBN (Ebook): 978-1-955737-76-0

University Professors Press
Colorado Springs, CO
www.universityprofessorspress.com

Cover Art by Nisha Gupta and Joseph Carreno (2016)
Cover Design by Laura Ross

Table of Contents

Preface

> Finding the center of strength within ourselves is in the long run the best contribution we can make to our fellow [human beings].
>
> ~ Rollo May[1]

The world is awhirl in extremes—extreme poverty, extreme wealth, extreme hatreds. The polarized mind[2] is at a dangerous peak, and so is the coarsening of culture, politicians, and governments. The digital mind is also at a perilous peak, and so is the addictive mind, the anxious mind, and the distracted mind. Many people are fed up with all these extremes.[3] They want major changes, and not just changes in one or two areas but across an entire way of living, especially as we get thrashed by this AI juggernaut that is looming. As a result, many people want to find a course between all these excesses, but they don't simply want mediocrity or "business as usual," as they (or their ancestors) experienced in the past. They want a between that sings, that can move, that can tap into the resources that have evolved, and that will keep evolving.

Accordingly, this is not a story about the "dull center" or "mindless mean." It's not a story about living a "flat" unadventurous life. Precisely the contrary! This is a story about an awakened and dynamic center, a vibrant center, pivoting to what is profound and meaningful at any given moment. This is a story about our capacity to choose and discern, to constrict and expand—not helter-skelter but as circumstances and moments suggest, and from a place that is alive, engaged, and maximally present. In contrast to rigid extremes and polarized ideologies, this story is about the urgency of a centered yet flexible alternative; a mindful alternative

At its core, this story is also about where we begin as separate yet connected creatures, and how to restore that sensibility—the sensibility of awe toward life. It's a story about learning to explore, take risks, experiment, and create, as well as restrain, confine, discipline, and defer—a story about engaging all our senses to the degree possible and transforming those senses into something practical, gratifying, and of social benefit.

Thus, throw away your stereotypes about balance, midpoints, and betweens and open to a fresh version of dynamic containment (playful constraint, humble daring, and reverent adventurousness). This version is animated, interactive, and invigorating. It has implications for fuller personal living for sure, but, equally, it has major consequences for getting along in the world. In fact, few places in the world have ever encouraged this kind of centering. The vast majority encourage either passivity or aggressiveness—or if not such extremism then blandness, superficiality. What I call the *vibrant center* has rarely been tried in communal living, either East or West, North or South. Why is this? Probably because it is unsettling for many people, an unsettlement that has vast consequences both for individuals and societies. Yet is it really worth trading off a little discomfort—uncertainty—for a "convenient" life, a life of simple answers and constrained horizons? A life where everything and everyone has their place and muddles along?

The vibrant center is not one of the quick fixes for our 21st century predicament; it is not a "seven simple steps" philosophy, although there are plenty of practical suggestions made in this book. Rather, it is a proposal for the long run, for the nourishing of society on many fronts. Short of that long-term approach, we target symptoms but not their roots; behaviors but not the inner lives that lead to the behaviors; individual transformation but not the transformation of the worlds individuals grow up in; positive thoughts but not the systems that too often tear those thoughts apart—in homes, schools, jobsites, places of worship, places of governance, places of news and entertainment. If we don't reach those latter realms, we continue placing band-aids on raging wounds. We lock in the status quo of bitterness, division, and war. And we forfeit the sense of agency for automation.

So get yourself ready to look at centering anew. Get yourself ready for a journey into the disquieting yet treasure-filled house of discovery and diversity, rigor and possibility.

I can't overstate the gravity of this venture, for the history of human destructiveness is the history of one-sidedness.

A Note About Method

This book is a philosophically and psychologically informed theory about what promotes a thriving individual and collective life. The theory of the "vibrant center" of consciousness, like all theories of optimal human functioning, is limited by evolving evidence, further need for exploration, and competing theories that may potentially prove more satisfactory to people.

That said, I want to be clear that this theory (or story) of the vibrant center is not a blueprint for a utopian society or a mathematically formulated law. It is a careful reflection based on my own personal and professional experience.[1] This experience draws chiefly from established existential–humanistic, psychoanalytic, and sociological sources, but also from anthropology, critical theory, and cross-cultural purviews. Further, this story is not a manifesto for some puritanical or sanitized view of life. To the contrary, the very definition of the vibrant center, which stresses *presence* (or really being there with one's whole-body awareness to the extent possible), *openness to experience* based on that presence, and *discernment* based on both that presence and openness, mitigates against such one-sidedness.

The method I use in this book therefore draws on my working definition of the vibrant center (described above) and the sources and testimonies that support it. The question as to whether I've succeeded in presenting my case is of course up to the reader. But I like to take my cue from another investigator of the human situation, Ernest Becker, who wrote: "The most that any one of us can...do is to fashion something... and drop it into the confusion;" to "make an offering of it, so to speak, to the life force."[2]

Introduction
The Vibrant Center of Living

I can't say it more bluntly: If you want to heal our broken society, elect leaders who promote dialogue not dogma. Elect leaders who are present, open-minded, and discerning.[1] This is our most urgent task. Our second most urgent task is to awaken that vibrant center[2] across every major sector of our society: from parenting to schools, from work and religious settings to diplomatic and legislative settings; otherwise we are simply polishing shipwrecks.

The second urgent task cannot manage very well without fulfilling the first major task; but the first urgent task cannot sustain itself without fulfilling the second urgent task. That's why this book addresses both tasks.

Let's begin with our first urgent task: The greatest danger to our society today is the political leadership that crushes dialogue. By "dialogue," which is another way to say "talking across the divides between people," I mean the core of what distinguishes democratic republics from dictatorships. And right now too many elements of the U.S. political leadership seem incapable of engaging in dialogue. Instead, they favor ranting, lying, manipulating, distorting, deceiving, dehumanizing, and extorting. They specialize in making "deals" when there are plentiful opportunities for listening, reflecting, and mutually deliberating. There also are plentiful opportunities for discussion and building foundations of trust. This is not always the case, to be sure. Sometimes quick and even transactional decisions need to be made, but part of the reason for that is the desperation brought about by the very mentality that crushes dialogue. This is the desperation of the ignored, the downtrodden, the resentful, and the sometimes violent. It is the desperation of a "dog-eat-dog" society that instead of reflecting on the deeper implications of treating people like objects or means to monetary ends plows ahead with top-down policies and neglect of communal needs. Thus. it is up to us, the people who are governed, to challenge the self-centered business model for living and install a new leadership that recognizes moral as well as pragmatic elements of governing. This is a leadership that places presence, deliberation, and dialogue at the core of governing so that communities and individuals can benefit alike. However, until that time we the people also need to pursue presence, deliberation, and dialogue lest the moral components of capitalism become extinguished from our daily life.

A world-renowned philosopher once said that we never step in the same river twice, implying that all is a flow and that no experience is an exact copy of a previous experience.

But is this true? I would say "yes" and "no." To be sure, it does appear that all is in flow, and no experience is an exact duplicate of an earlier experience. But it's also true that the "river" we step into is all of a piece. Our present experience (flow) is impacted by all those experiences (flows) that preceded it, and equally, all those that are ahead of it. The river we step into, the so-called constant flow, is but a part of all—one river and one flow. It is separate but related.

This is a really hard lesson for human beings to learn. There ain't no simple answer. One size doesn't fit all, and the sooner we get that the better off we'll be. We need, at last, to recognize and make the best of the nuggets of truth in many positions. This is a lesson many of us have failed to learn for millennia. In my study of dominant societies (or "power centers") since the beginning of recorded time, what I call the polarized mind, or the mindset that fixates on single points of view to the utter exclusion of competing points of view, is a major affliction.[3] And this is true East and West, North and South, and regardless of political party.

Today we are in a similar knot. In fact, it's a scarier knot because today the dominant powers have access to technology that could decimate our species in seconds. This means that the enormous stakes of life today must be matched by an equally powerful mind- and heart-set. They must be matched by a way of life and form of governance that recognizes the stakes of a polarized mind and that works tirelessly to depolarize and revitalize the condition of humanity.

In this book, I describe the need for a philosophy, movement, and political party that firmly position themselves on the accumulated—and hard-won!—wisdom of millennia. This wisdom calls for us to confront fear-driven impulses and draw on the center or "pivot point" of our many-sided lives.[4] This approach, which I call the vibrant center, urges us to slow down, to pause, and to deeply reflect on the direction of our lives, *while we have the time* to engage in this capacity and before it's too late. The approach also calls for lifestyles and forms of governance that support people—especially marginalized and disadvantaged people—to engage this capacity.

In the pages to follow, I will do my level best to outline a vision of the vibrant center that links child-rearing, education, work, religious and spiritual settings and governance into a dynamic whole, a necessary whole. I will also sketch out a vision of a political party—a Vibrant Center party—that some readers may wish to translate into a reality. Hopefully, they will be in a much better position than I to formulate, organize, and implement some of the ideas I put forth in this book. Finally, I will explore in detail how an "awe-based," vibrantly centered world could arise (see also Appendix A). I will draw on the stories of both "everyday" people and luminaries who embody those latter qualities and offer them as prototypes, resilient exemplars who may "seed" the world to come.

To sum, this book is an informed yet provisional roadmap for personal and collective well-being. It is based on many years of study, discussion, and living. In some sense, I am attempting to renew Abraham Maslow's quest to explore what is best in humanity, yet with the urgency and socio-political relevance of our age. The vibrant center is neither self nor communally focused, but a meld of both. It is the actualizing of humanity for the betterment of humanity—a task of which most of us, I contend, would approve. That said, I am not certain of any of this. But what I am more sure of is that if we are to make it as a society—let alone species--a sobering change is needed. That change must draw from recognized sources of historical wisdom, even if that wisdom has never really had a chance to shine like it needs to—it has to—today.

Chapter 1

The Vibrant Center of Parenting

From the moment we are born, we are propelled into chaos. We shift from a place of warmth and security to coldness and disarray, from solidity and certainty to groundlessness and confusion. Arguably, all the major adult fears are rooted in this helplessness and groundlessness: abandonment, rejection, insignificance, loss of control, invisibility, homelessness, death and so on.[1] The question is: How are we met at this moment of cleavage—both by our caretakers and the society that receives us? How are we seen, heard, and introduced by our new overseers? Are we viewed as intruders and puppets to be used or as treasures and participants to be welcomed? Are we bombarded with prejudices and prohibitions, or are we engaged with delight and curiosity? Are we shut down or embraced, resonated with? Do we learn fear and hatred of the unknown—the foreign and the "other"—or do we learn to wonder about them, discover something about them?

Do we learn to make ourselves small and inconspicuous or great and unbounded? Or do we learn how to work with these capacities, to see the value in both conforming at times and venturing out at other times; living carefreely and heeding limits?[2] These are but a few of the questions I commend parents to consider as they accompany a child into the world. And they are a few of the questions I believe our society should consider as it guides parents and children at this pivotal fork in the road in their life-journeys.

Finding the Grace-Points in Polarities

When I was a youth (I'm now a youthful 69), I used to think that rules were mostly nonsense, an excuse for adults to silence everyone and make everything calm. They certainly weren't helpful when it came to my voracious desires to play, to watch my favorite television shows, to eat my favorite candy bars, and to stay up all night joking with friends at sleepovers.

The problem with rules got more serious when I became a teenager and was getting interested in "hot" dates and finding places to "make out," dance at late-night bars, or become mesmerized at midnight movies. When I joined the high school swim team, I encountered rules like I never had before: wake up at six in the morning, get your butt to school on the coldest winter days (this was Cleveland), and jump into bone-chilling, chlorine-bathed water. Then, no matter how sleepy I (like the rest of the team) was, I was told to swim at least a mile, and if I moved too slowly the coach yelled at me, or maybe even threw a kickboard at me as "incentive." Then I was told to return to the pool after school and repeat the whole damn process again for another hour and a half! "Why am I torturing myself?" I wondered.

On the academic side, rules got even more oppressive when they dampened my desire to explore nonrequired books or writing ideas, and when strict views about grammar and literary style as well as practical content such as math or science seemed to encroach on my imagination and creativity.

And what about all those civilities I was bombarded with as a kid—like "have a nice day," or "be a good boy" or "be a gentleman." Did I really have to hear those without end? Then there were the firm boundaries around self-control like: remember to "drive safely," "don't be a wild man," or "don't go in that neighborhood at night." Moreover, did I really need my teacher telling me I couldn't talk too loud or laugh at a friend's joke in class? Did I really need my mother telling me to tuck my shirt in every day, or to wear clothes that match?

And when I began my university years, did I really need to be told that if I didn't learn history I'd be condemned to repeat the past, that math and statistics were essential to a good grounding in psychology (my major at the time), that "practice makes perfect," that "I'm too good to write like a high school drop-out" (which is what one of my mentors told me when I started graduate school), or that I need to learn the basics before I will amount to anything?

Well, I've had a lifetime of issues with these dos and don'ts, and I'm not done yet. I'm sure many of us feel this way. But what I do realize—and I think many in our modern or, better, "postmodern" era have been awakened to—is that as much as those old sayings frustrated the hell out of many of us, many were also critical at some level. Consider, for example, how the amplification of recklessness at the highest levels of government appear to be tearing at the fabric of human decency in our society as a whole. This problem is exemplified by the philosophy of tech moguls and some of the richest men in the world when they speak of "moving fast and breaking things." One of those moguls, Elon Musk, seemed to embody that philosophy with his intense—and some would say destructive--campaign to reduce the size of the federal government.[3] The problem of human decency is also illustrated by an official U.S. Justice Department memo that called a reporter a "dope" for asking a question and U.S. President Trump's characterization of Somali immigrants as "garbage."[4]

This period we are laboring with reflects the iconic poem by William Butler Yeats like few others:

> Turning and turning in the widening gyre
> The falcon cannot hear the falconer;
> Things fall apart; the centre cannot hold;
> Mere anarchy is loosed upon the world,
> The blood-dimmed tide is loosed, and everywhere
> The ceremony of innocence is drowned;

> The best lack all conviction, while the worst
> Are full of passionate intensity.[5]

Perhaps it takes a crisis like we have today to realize how rules and boundaries are as integral to human vitality as are freedom and discovery—and if we glorify one pole to the exclusion of the other, we court disaster. If we leave out our needs for humility and sensitivity, for example, then we foster coarseness (and too often) violence. Correspondingly, if we leave out our needs for individuality and choice, we promote passivity and conformity.

Much of the task of growing up focuses on reconciling diverse and sometimes contradictory points of view. This means that much of the task of good parenting is about helping kids face these varying standpoints, learn how to deal with them, and, often enough, learn how to live with them even if they are unsettling and sometimes downright infuriating.

Where is the line between optimal and suboptimal support of this approach? There's obviously no clear line, but what does seem clear is that parents need to spend time with their kids, and not just quantity of time but attuned quality time. It means parents and the system that surrounds them need to ensure that they have that time and can develop that attunement. It means that parental support programs are essential, but it also means that parents need to make time to be present and converse with their kids, and set firm boundaries when their kids are in danger.

The renowned child development researcher, Diana Baumrind, confirms these multifaced parenting skills. She distinguishes among parenting styles—permissive, authoritarian, and authoritative—and finds the latter optimal.[6] Permissive parenting gives kids the message that they can express themselves as they please, absent of real-life consequences, while authoritarian parenting robs kids of their sense of agency. Authoritative parenting weaves into the vibrant center of these extremes, providing abundant room for self-expression but also clear feedback about the consequences of that expression, along with realistic boundaries that support them in navigating life.

Awe for Life at the Heart of Parenting

The sense of awe—humility and wonder, adventure toward life—is a key dimension of both vibrant-centered and authoritative parenting. This underappreciated sensibility is critical not only for the development of children but for the development of their world. If you are a parent or even caretaker, can you see how vital it is to approach a child with genuine curiosity about their lives? Do you realize how profoundly that curiosity sparks the child's curiosity and freedom to wonder, wander, and discover?

Awe is a birthright that we all probably experience from the start, but it is also the natural foundation for resilience. It supports the child to learn close up how small they are in comparison to the enormity of existence. It gives the child a playground for possibilities because it avoids pre-defining those possibilities, hardening them and categorizing them like a robot. It gives the child *room* instead of imposing rooms on them; and it enables the child to learn about their own vulnerability and the need to care for that vulnerability. Likewise, it enables children to empathize to some degree with parental rules and to see that ideally those rules are there to protect, not to punish.[7]

On the other hand, parental wonder, boldness, and risk-taking empowers children to tap into the vastness around them and to challenge their vulnerability. The wonder part of awe helps children to see that they too can have an impact on the world, that discovery, creativity, and feeling like they are part of something much greater than themselves can greatly nourish their world.

Based on everything I've witnessed, the awesomeness of life can be felt in the most ordinary circumstances.[8] Throwing a ball to your kid on a sunny day, taking your kid out to a park or forest, swimming with them in a lake or ocean, bringing them together with friends or family, having a picnic or cookout with them, taking them for a walk or ride into the city, seeing plays or movies together, reading together, playing games or sports together, traveling to new destinations, touring museums, sharing in great meals and conversations, singing or playing music together, or just appreciating the beauty of hanging out together, whether in nature or in a coffee shop—all these can be opportunities for awe and the discovery that awe is an ongoing possibility, an ongoing nectar of living.

Of course, kids don't always feel so awesome, and neither do parents. Poverty, illness, physical and emotional limitations can all derail the accessibility of awe. Living in the midst of war and violence makes the attainment of awe almost ludicrous. And yet we do know that people like the psychiatrist Viktor Frankl experienced flashes of awe while observing the Bavarian mountains on a transport train to Auschwitz—and even while in the death camp when he mustered the ability to visualize his smiling wife. We also know that astrophysicist Stephen Hawking was able to maintain contact with the awesomeness of the universe and the great questions about the universe while in the grip of the devastating illness ALS (also known as Lou Gehrig's Disease). We likewise know that the poet and novelist Maya Angelou, who suffered rape as a seven-year-old and countless encounters with racism, found awe through reading about others, such as Harlem Renaissance writer Langston Hughes. Hughs also experienced the torments of dehumanization and yet found ways to express and transform that anguish into consciousness-expanding narrative. Many similar examples can be cited among rebellious yet centered activists, such as Martin Luther King inspiring nonviolent protests on behalf of the civil rights of American blacks, Nelson Mandela promoting dialogue and humanism for the emancipation of South African blacks over the course of a 27-year prison sentence, and Mahatma Gandhi dedicating a lifetime to the nonviolent overthrow of British rule in India.

These are extraordinary people to be sure. But they also show us what is possible, as I will elaborate later in the book. Even in the most depraved circumstances, these exemplars give us hints about how we can use our own freedom to imagine, wonder, and create or at least temper our painful circumstances and enter into the "more" of who we are, what the world can be. Parents need to convey that sensibility to their kids *while at the same time* being realistic about the challenges they and their children face. We will address a vibrant-center approach to the wider systems we tangle with—namely, religion, culture, and politics in chapters 4 through 7 as these are obviously crucial to the global facilitation of an awe-based sensibility.

Critical Thinking Through Conversation is Imperative

When I was about 7 years old, I joined a group of kids chasing after a learning-disabled kid of color. The group was making fun of that kid because of his skin color and the fact that he had trouble talking. It was a horrible and rare episode for me, but I guess I just wanted to be accepted by the "cool" kids at that moment and was afraid of being left out or put down because I didn't go along. Maybe I was afraid of being mocked myself as the only Jewish kid in the neighborhood predominated by Catholics and Protestants. It is true that I too had been mocked at times, and even spat on for being a "Christ Killer" and for being different. Some idiot even painted a big black Swastika on a wall of our garage one morning. Accordingly, some very core wounds drove me to be a joiner that afternoon, as I blended in with the gang and probably mimicked some of their repulsive language.

Was I unconscious of what I was doing? To some degree I would have to say "yes." Did I have choice? Also yes, I had a vague sense that what I was doing was contemptible and yet I turned away from this choice; I turned away from reflection and caved in to my need to be accepted and seen as OK. The alternative on the other hand, was probably associated with being stripped of my identity, of being seen as a "nobody," or worse, another monstrosity, like that kid we were chasing.

That said, an unexpected thing happened moments into this calamity. My father ran into the street, grabbed me by the arm and brought me back to our house. He was fuming but it was a controlled rage that he clearly recognized, as I was soon to recognize, was absolutely necessary to turn this incident from a nightmare of assaults into a life-turning moment of illumination. It was one of the most important life-discoveries of my childhood, and that's why I remember it so vividly. Carefully and yet firmly, dad proceeded to strike me one or two times on my butt, and then sat me down and had a concerted conversation with me. His look told me how disappointed he was with my decision to join the gang in the street, but then he fired away a series of questions at me that conveyed not only his seriousness but the seriousness of the moment and challenged me to look squarely at what I had done. His first question, I believe, was "How would you feel if you were Jerry X (a pseudonym for the boy being chased), and a gang of kids suddenly came at you and started calling you names, chased you through the streets, and threatened you with being beaten to the ground?" I'm sure this startled me and got me to think about the horror of that position and how unfair it would be. "How would you feel," he continued, "if you were a darker skin color and people hated you just for that? Or for being slow or slurring your words?" The deeper he dug into the situation the heavier my heart felt, and the heavier I felt about what I had just participated in. "How did you feel when kids spat at you for being Jewish, or when they painted a Nazi sign on our garage," he continued. "Could it be that Jerry felt something similar?" I'm sure I nodded at that point and was intensely reviewing all the points my dad was bringing up. More thoughts welled up in me based on our conversation:

like what does it mean to be different, just how bad is that, and why is it so bad? What does it mean to be accepted? Accepted for what? A crowd of ignorant bullies who degraded people? A life of hate and violence? What does it mean to feel superior? A temporary feeling of being better than others, but what is "better?" Being angry, hateful, and bitter? Being mean? Stepping on others' rights? These questions led to a flood of other questions. Why do I need to be superior to someone else? To get a fleeting glimpse of power? To counter-balance feeling weak and unimportant? To be like a feelingless robot?

Now I should be clear that my dad very rarely got angry like this; and he rarely hounded me with so many urgent questions. He was generally a very warm and loving figure in my life—and he rarely if ever had spanked me. But that afternoon was different, and made all the more so in the background of what I knew about my dad and how much I admired him for his socially just stands, and his consistent openness to inquiry, mutuality, and discovery.

My dad's integrity therefore made that afternoon all the more noteworthy and all the more an occasion for pausing, reflecting, and reassessing. That afternoon was probably my first major experiential encounter with critical thinking and the value of deep, methodical reevaluation of a pivotal event in my life. From that encounter with my dad, I believe I learned the necessity of a more thoughtful, morally conscious life, a life driven not by gangs or crowds or even parental commands per se but by my own conscience, my own heartfelt view of what it means to live with dignity in this world and to support greater dignity in others.

What I'm basically getting at here is the urgency of instilling critical thinking in children, from the earliest ages. These are the seeds of the much subtler reflection and discernment we learn as adolescents and adults. They are the seedbeds of what we need a lot more of in schools, as we will discuss, and among peers, politicians, and social systems. If we don't start these inquiry processes early on, we are much more prone to live fear-driven lives, conformity-driven lives where media and fashion and autocrats rule our days—as distinct from more or less our own agencies, our own centers, and our own consciences fueling our life-paths.

I would also go so far as to say that my early experiences with critical thinking (and feeling) set the foundation for me to be wary of three crucial psychological barriers to a more vibrant center: *conflation* or the equation of one person with a whole group of people or one idea with an entire ideology, as happens when we become prejudiced against given ethnicities or worldviews; *confirmation bias* or the tendency to see what we want to see based on our prejudices, as happens when we go about looking for and finding something negative about those we oppose; and *cognitive dissonance* or the tendency to defend one's view regardless of the evidence (or lack thereof) supporting it, as I demonstrated initially when I overrode my doubts and joined the gang of kids despite repeated indications of how contemptible we all were. Thus conflation, confirmation bias, and cognitive dissonance are big deals. Why don't our educational systems reinforce our knowledge about these social plagues?

In addition to discovering the above plagues, I also learned the rudiments of a more philosophical approach to my own and others' lives. I learned, for example, to look more closely at the assumptions, or what philosophers call premises, on which I based my abusive actions. I began to see that my behavior and mindset were fixed on being accepted by my peers rather than what was humane in that assaultive episode. I also began to see how I was fixated more on popular prejudices against skin color or ways of speaking than I was on the "more" of who Jerry was. In so many ways, this more would have shown Jerry to be a kind and gentle soul, a playful and sociable kid. Thus, my lack of awareness about the assumptions I began with took me straight into contemptuous acts, mindless and heartless acts, whereas learning about the distortion and bankruptcy of those assumptions provided fresh inroads into broader and more attuned assumptions that brought much more fulfillment for me and, I'm sure, Jerry, as we gradually began to reassess each other and find livelier ways to relate to each other. The awakening to bankrupt assumptions also gave me a more critical stance toward my accomplices who partook in the depraved act. It spurred me to speak up against such involvements and to learn more about why I and others act as we do, even when we have a sense deep down that we're doing something reprehensible. These trains of thought and feeling were also seedlings for my future career as a psychotherapist and certainly added to my interest in psychology.

Correspondingly, I began to learn about the difference between group behavior and behavior we're inclined to when we face someone one on one, when we actually make contact with another person. I learned that the contrast was stark. The shift from simple reactions (prejudices) groups tend to harbor with the more nuanced responses (humanizations) that person-to-person contacts tend to evoke can change one's whole outlook on cultures, societies, and even the world. It was a sense of being less driven by fears and transmitted dogmas and more driven by curiosities and evolving discoveries.

What then can we learn about the vibrant center from this specific episode in my life? I would say first and foremost we learn, if we need to again, how readily we are thrown off our centers by peer pressure and group consensus. Underlying my own compulsion to join the hostile group were common yet very primal terrors that many if not most children—and adults—share: the terror of rejection, abandonment, unimportance; feeling lost, overlooked, hated, unloved, isolated; and maybe even being killed or physically injured. The upshot is that these fears relate directly to the core wounds of being born and the foreignness of our condition. They are unaddressed elements of our groundlessness and helplessness before the vastness of existence, our earliest experience of separation, and our ejection from the womb. All of these call for the need to be met and supported so that we can find our center of wonder and discovery in the midst of groundlessness and helplessness. In the absence of that meeting, we are left with the fear-based prejudices of others and our own undeveloped abilities to confront and work through those prejudices.

My dad, it seems to me, was able to succeed at meeting me at that crucial juncture of my life. His stance exemplified a vibrant center. He brought concerted presence to the seriousness of my actions, openness to discussing my struggle, and firmness or discernment about the necessity for me to confront my struggle, to see and feel what I was doing to myself as well as others. His mixture of seriousness, care, and challenging conversation jarred me awake and created a lasting memory about the depth of our humanity and the need to be humane. Although I am skeptical about it as a rule, even his light spanking impressed upon me the gravity of the situation both for the victim Jerry but also for me and my world. From then on, there was no easy way for me to distance myself from hateful acts like the one I got caught up in or to separate hate for mere differences in another from hate for mere differences within myself. I was compelled to face the different and foreign, and from there to realize their possibilities for a richer and more diversified life.

Meaning in Life

The development of a vibrant center is integral to cultivating meaning in life. It is very difficult to feel a sense of deep meaning if one is not able to be present, open, and discerning. Just consider this for a moment. If I can't pause, focus my attention, or bring my whole body experience to an event or relationship, what chance does it have of being genuinely significant? What chance does it have of being more than a fleeting whim or high? What chance does it have of being more than a surface glimpse? Very little, I would say. Likewise, if I can't be open to an event or relationship, if I can't wonder about it, be curious and interested in what I might discover about it, it's very unlikely that I will view it as meaningful. It is more likely that it will be mechanical, routine, lifeless. Correspondingly, if I come at the thing or person with all kinds of fears, assumptions, and biases—many of which were carried over from my family, culture, or unaddressed traumas—it's very likely that I will experience that thing or person in a narrow or trivial way, completely overlooking possibilities for new insights, directions, or even surprises. Finally, if I lack discernment about the person or thing I'm experiencing what possible priority could it have in my life? Why would that person or thing stand out from any other person or thing? What significance does flitting about from place to place, person to person, or object to object have for a fuller and more gratifying life? We see this problem with kids who are over-indulged, for example, and provided with too many toys, too many privileges, or too many rewards; they rarely seem to learn what the *best* people, places, or things are or the most meaningful directions to pursue.

Therapy and Mentoring

When we speak of finding our centers through caretakers, we also need to speak of therapy and mentoring. We need to speak, as previously suggested, of the "helpful witnesses" that come across our paths beyond our parents—beyond our cultures even—who provide a centered window into who we are and who we can be at our core. Langston Hughes and other black artists provided such a window for Maya Angelou, but there are so many others—including myself—who have been lifted from the scrap-heap of trauma by neighbors, teachers, friends, lovers, athletic and artistic heroes, coaches, aunts, uncles, grandparents, and, of course, physicians and therapists. These are folks that point us to our cores, to the heart of what deeply matters, and the pathways that can lead us to live what deeply matters. They are broken people who found great strength, in part because they were broken and very likely helped themselves to break through to blocked-off parts of themselves, the "more" of who they can be.

When we speak of our center, we speak of connection—both inner and outer. We speak of generations of seekers, strugglers, battlers who recognized that we are both wounded and resilient but that we have some range of choice within that tension and the mental and physical capacities to exercise those choices, even in the most dire circumstances—short of death, of course.

While some say that there is no center or core, that there is no "self" as such, I do sympathize with this view. We are "multitudes" as Walt Whitman stated in *Leaves of Grass*. Life is "impermanence," as Buddhists (and deconstructionists!) would say,[9] and on some level, I believe they're right. We, like the universe, are in constant motion, constant change, and constant uncertainty. But for all that we are also flesh and blood creatures with only so much time. We are *constellated* by physiology, genes, cultural and historical circumstances, parental engagements, friends, communities, and some rather elusive, profoundly mysterious sense of self and the intimacies that attend that sense of self. No, I am not "Kirk Schneider" in any hardened mechanical sense. I am not a label or thing. But I am a constellation of Kirk Schneider, just as the planets in our solar system are a constellation of orbits in the universe, unique to the universe, or likely so, just as the markings of a leaf or snowflake are constellations unique so far as we know to those particular entities.

So, insofar as my life-experience has taught me both locally and globally, we humans are ever-evolving, ever-reverberating energies that are also intimately bonded in ways that perhaps only poets can begin to articulate. I think here of Pascal and "the heart has its reasons that reason knows not," or the old adage that "it's better to have loved and lost than never to have loved at all." These sayings or "pointings" suggest that experientially we live in a paradoxical condition of unfathomable cosmic evolution and inner depth but also of "soul" and "heart."[10] We throw our arms up in despair. "What does it all mean?" But we also have the choice and, indeed, the vision to embrace that so-called futility, to see it as part of an even larger pathway: our participation in mystery. As Heschel puts it: "Reverence is one of [humanity's] answers to the presence of mystery...it does not rush to be spoken.... In such moments.... all we want is to pause, to be still, that the moment will last."[11]

This wisdom is the cornerstone of what therapists and mentors can provide for us, often beyond our conventional educations. Great therapists and mentors convey to us that sense of gratification when we have touched something deeply significant about our relationships to others, our creative possibilities, our possibilities for living with a richer awe-based outlook. This outlook is not at all some absolute or all-encompassing "truth," but it is *imperative for us.* It is worth staking our very lives to realize. And isn't that enough? Do we really need absolutes to sanctify it? I don't believe so; we need centering to keep it alive, vibrant, and relevant to our times.[12]

Consider Maya Angelou's opening lines about her childhood catastrophe, "free fall"—as well as awakening:

> When I was seven and a half, I was raped....Now to show you how out of evil there can come good, in those five years [following her rape] I read every book in the Black school library; I read all the books I could get from the White school library....And out of this evil I was able to draw from human thought, human disappointments and triumphs, enough to triumph myself.[13]

"It is doubtful," states Rollo May, "whether anyone really begins to live, that is, to affirm and choose [their] existence, until [they have] frankly confronted the terrifying fact that they could wipe out their existence but *chooses* not to."[14]

As in the case of Maya Angelou, the best therapists and mentors help us move beyond encrusted ways of viewing ourselves and the world and become open not only to how we are presently living but to how we have been imprisoning ourselves in familiar yet tormenting patterns. They help us to realize not only how we desire to live, but also how we are *willing* to live and, indeed, are capable of living by breaking out of those patterns. Heschel writes:

> The world in which we live is a... cage within a maze, high as our mind, wide as our power of will, long as our life-span. Those who have never reached the rails or seen what is beyond the cage know of no freedom to dream of and are willing to rise and fight for civilizations that come and go and sink into the abyss of oblivion, an abyss which they never fill.[15]

Finding our vibrant center means the pivot point from which we can "see" the cage and maze we live within and recognize the choice we have to reach the rails of that cage and maze. It means that freedom, or what I call "life-enhancing anxiety," resides on the other side of the cage and somewhere fulfilling within the maze. It means that we have discovered this trajectory, and often that a "witness"—a therapist, mentor, or ideally a parent—has supported us to pursue it, in spite of and even in light of its perils.

The vibrant center, or pivot point of life, then is critical to a life that can take time to build itself up and flourish. It's integral to making sound and gratifying decisions and to adapting to a variety of circumstances that will inevitably cross its path. So why do we so rarely prize such a life in our society? Why do we so rarely see such a life as the prototype of either childhood or adulthood, education or work, religion or legislative action?

Instead, we see prototypes of "efficiency," conformity, adjustment—or worse, reactivity, embitterment, violence, which are overcompensation for feeling helpless and groundless. This is what we desperately need to explore, and will do so as we look closer at the systems that perpetuate polarization as distinct from centeredness. We begin with the educational system, which has a very mixed record when it comes to centeredness.

Chapter 2

The Vibrant Center of Education

Supporting Kids to be Present, Open, and Discerning; Touching on the Awesomeness of Life

When is education—school—most vibrant? When do kids become excited about learning, thinking, inquiring? And when does education have a meaningful impact on life—a gratifying life? I can't answer for every kid, of course, and I don't have the expertise to lay out a formal curriculum. But I can speak from my experience as a kid, and later therapist and educator.

So here are some reflections. Start with structure but don't drop variety. Give kids a safe and supportive environment. Provide them with sensible boundaries (e.g., you can't hit or dehumanize others). But within that framework teach kids how to be present, open, and discerning. In other words send the message about how important their classroom is for living, not just going through routines. That means inspiring play, of course. but also challenging kids to think and to channel their emotions. What do I mean by challenging kids to think? I mean gradually presenting kids with real-life problems such as: What makes them happy? What makes them sad? What do they fear? What do they love? What makes a good community? What makes a miserable community? How do they handle frustration? What do they do when they feel put down or rejected? How do they repair broken relationships? When do they repair such relationships?

Then in later years, perhaps upper-level high school and initial college years, encourage questions like: What is the definition of being human in the face of challenges like abortion, AI, robotics? What is the definition of a man, woman? Can we expand our definition of gender to include transgender and nonbinary individuals? What are the implications of this expansion for everyday life? What is the definition of race and who determines it? What role should multicultural viewpoints play in U.S. classrooms, syllabuses? What are the criteria for science, especially a science of persons? What are the criteria for truth? What is evil, what is moral, and who decides? What are basic human rights and how far should they extend (e.g., for healthcare, education, childcare, self-protection, freedom of speech, freedom of the press, freedom of religion)? What is the role of a federal government versus state or local government, and are governments even necessary? What is the optimal government for a multicultural society such as ours? How should we treat fellow animals and the natural world? How should we treat criminals and the mentally disturbed? What are optimal policies toward immigrants? And perhaps the most important question for many kids: What is the awesome life?

Correspondingly, and perhaps by middle school, begin to teach kids about the *premises* of people's viewpoints. This is perhaps the most pivotal yet underappreciated theme in the entire educational process, and emphatically why a class in philosophy is imperative for childhood maturation. Exploring the premises of viewpoints is quite literally pivotal because it teaches children to stand in the center of issues and carefully weigh their value. At its best, it teaches kids not only to think through the relevance, timeliness, and truth of a particular view but to feel and imagine what it might be like to take up a given view. This is where it is helpful not only to "talk about" the pros and cons of various standpoints but to role play them, learn about them in real-life settings like field trips, and experience them in their day-to-day lives. I have to admit that I probably learned as much about cities, art, music, archeology, and even diverse cultures from field trips as I did from hours of classroom discussion about these matters. And I know that my "senior project"—working as a collections agent at a mortgage company in downtown Cleveland—taught me more about the business world, civic engagement, and class conflict than any of the classes that touched on these subjects. There is little doubt that such "real life" exposures are critical to young peoples' formation of ideas about how to live, where to live, what to contribute to society, and what to resist in society.

The Experiential Democracy Dialogue

Another "tool" that can facilitate this exploration is for children in upper grades to learn a form of engagement I call the "Experiential Democracy Dialogue" (or EDD).[1] The EDD is a one-on-one approach that aims to "humanize" otherwise devaluing or reductionist conversations between people who hold conflicting cultural or political views. It can be especially helpful for kids to refine their skills for critical thinking skills and their understanding of the premises on which their viewpoints are based. But the EDD is not just an intellectual tool; it involves one's holistic experience of the identified "other," supporting the partners to understand each other emotionally and imaginatively as well as cognitively.

Before elaborating on the EDD, however, one note of caution is in order. It is not for everyone, and some people, especially those from minoritized communities, may need preparatory work before engaging in it. By this I mean that some people could be hesitant to engage in a dialogue about race or gender if their dialogue partner is representative of a group that has consistently devalued them. Or if the dialogue partner was known to have directly harmed someone themselves due to their social position or identity. How could one trust that their dialogue partner, for example, an upper-class white male, would not—wittingly or unwittingly—reactivate power imbalances that have proved deeply disturbing to the given individual? How could a black individual who has continually been viewed as "less than" in a majority white world experience the safety to be open and vulnerable with a white individual from a completely contrasting background? While the dialogue ground rules can help to some degree in such situations—as we shall see—they also may not be nearly adequate to address the intensity of the situation. In such cases, some form of preparatory work from the start—such as acknowledgment of the power imbalances or engagement in restorative justice, or a similar process—may be in order.

Moreover, it is incumbent on the facilitator of the dialogue to have an awareness of these multicultural dynamics.[2] For example, it is well known in the conflict mediation community that the provision of safe, structured formats is essential to successful engagement. We have learned this over some very hard lessons through the years. One of the prime instances of these lessons were the "Racial Confrontation" workshops held between the (mostly white) leaders of Esalen Institute and the regional Black Panther party in 1968.[3] Put succinctly, the well-intended dialogue ended up in a shouting match;[4] and while the basis for this debacle is still being debated, the lack of preparation and ground rules would seem to be strong candidates. These could either have 1) precluded the meeting and resultant brawl from proceeding altogether; or 2) provided the guardrails necessary for the dialogue partners to at least be heard by one another, and perhaps even "seen" to the degree that some sliver of common ground may have been achievable. In any case, these are all lessons well worth noting as one proceeds through the remainder of this section.

Accordingly, the aim of the EDD is to learn about and understand one's dialogue partner and not to assume knowledge about them or impose one's view on them, as is typical of dialogues that deteriorate very quickly. While the EDD in theory can be engaged with two mature individuals, I highly recommend, especially for children, that it be facilitated by a teacher who is well versed in mediation skills as well as the EDD format. It is also helpful initially to demonstrate the approach in front of a class. This way, children have an experiential as well as cognitive sense of how to practice it themselves (later in the class and under the supervision of a facilitator). I strongly advise that the demonstration partners meet with the facilitator prior to the class demonstration so that they can be better prepared both for the EDD format and the degree of composure that's necessary in working through the format.

Here is an overview of the EDD format:

> The Experiential Democracy Dialogue proceeds with two partners holding conflicting cultural or political views. The following overview comprises the ground rules, the setup (for the partners to select the topic of their conversation), and dialogue phases 1–6:

Summary of the Experiential Democracy Dialogue for Two[5]

Ground Rules

- We are here to understand others and explain our views, not to convince others to change their mind.
- Let's each of us try to speak for ourselves and not try to speak for or represent any outside group.
- Let's stick to the spirit of the activities designed for each phase of the dialogue.
- Otherwise, this is standard stuff we all know: taking turns, not interrupting others, listening to others, being respectful (e.g., as in no eye-rolling, or loud sighs when someone is speaking).
- In other words, bring your best selves to a difficult conversation. Try your best to come from a place of curiosity, respect (if not for the partner's belief than at least for their willingness to engage in civil, present dialogue with you), and openness.

Dialogue Set-Up (2 Minutes)
Partners decide on a topic and the liberal or conservative (or other polarized) positions they'll respectively take. Some partners may need to role play someone they know who conflicts with them. Example topics:

- How do you feel society is dealing with political polarization, the pandemic, racism, the economic crisis, or other crises of your choosing? (choose one issue)
- How are *you* dealing with political polarization, the pandemic, racism, the economic crisis, or other crises of your choosing? (choose one issue)
  Please remember to adhere to the Ground Rules

Dialogue Phases
Phase One: Visualizing the Dialogue *(4 Minutes)*
Each partner begins by silently visualizing what it might be like to engage in (a given) dialogue with the other partner.
- (2 mins.) Each partner is invited to observe, without fixating on, the feelings, sensations, and thoughts that come up when visualizing the dialogue with the other. (Simply acknowledge and do your best to co-exist with the tensions and differences that emerge.)
- (2 mins.) Each partner is invited to envision—clear a space for—the humanity of their partner, their flesh and blood humanness, vulnerability, and personal story beyond the initial "stamp" you impose on them

Phase Two: Background *(10 Minutes, 5 for each partner)*
Invitation for each dialogue partner to describe their background and summarize very briefly what it was like growing up *and* how their family/culture treated the ideological "other" as related to the issue at hand. (Thus, if the topic is on a political difference, talk about how that political difference—such as gun rights or racism—was handled by caretakers. Or what if any critical incidents in your life shaped

your view of such issues? These questions elaborate the context for one's perspective.)

Phase Three: Taking a Stance *(12 Minutes)*
Invitation for each partner to tell, as mindfully and heartfully as possible, his/her "side" of an issue without interruption, followed by paraphrases of what was heard by the listener, with chance for correction.

- (4 mins.) Speaking partner describes stance.
- (2 mins.) Listening partner reflects back what they heard, and speaking partner corrects them if needed. (6 mins. total)
- (6 mins.) Speaker and listener switch roles.

Phase Four: Identifying, Correcting, Admitting Stereotypes *(12 Minutes)*
Identifying perceived stereotyping of one's position, correction of that view, and identifying nuggets of truth in the stereotype. (6 mins. for each partner)

- (2 mins.) Speaking partner identifies perceived stereotyping of their position by those critical of them, for example, "naïve" if liberal or "dogmatic" if conservative.
- (2 mins.) Speaking partner presents a correction of that view.
- (2 mins.) Speaking partner identifies nuggets of truth to the stereotype.
- (6 mins.) Speaker and listener switch roles.

Phase Five: Asking a Policy Question *(10 Minutes)*
In this phase, partners ask each other one question about their respective stances. It is vital that the question be as neutral and nonpartisan as possible—just a straightforward policy question; no "gotcha," accusatory, or sarcastic questions. Ask with genuine curiosity (e.g., "Given the level of violence in our society, can you help me to understand your position on your

right to openly carry a gun?" or "Can you tell me more about your belief that a white person who never owned slaves should pay reparations to people of color?")

- (5 mins.) Each partner asks one question of the other, who then responds regarding their respective stance.
- (5 mins.) Questioner and responder switch roles.

Phase Six: Discovery/Results *(10 Minutes)*
In this final phase dialogue, partners take time to reflect on and convey what they learned about themselves, their partner, and the relationship they have built. The respective partners also discuss what, if any, common ground has been achieved and what if any steps they will take in the future based on their dialogue.

- (5 mins.) Each partner conveys what was discovered during the dialogue. (Remember to stay in character if one is role playing a position.)
- (5 mins.) Partners switch roles.

Some questions to guide your discussion: Did you feel heard? Did your partner relate to your narrative? What was learned both about your partner and yourself? Was there any common ground achieved? Action plans? Possibilities for carrying the dialogues further?

Again, there are so many premises to examine critically today—from what makes a given individual or culture healthy, to the value of a democratic society; from the role of centralized power to legislative representation; from free speech to the use of guns and the military; and from the need for technological and material well-being to the need for psychological and spiritual well-being.

The Call for Critical Inquiry

Every one of these issues—and those discussed above—could take weeks, months, and even years to parse out, especially if they are substantively engaged and inclusive of thoughts, feelings, imaginings, life-experience, conversations, and classroom activities. The encounter with these issues could also be integrated into a range of areas of study—from sociology to history, biology to economics, and literature to the visual arts. But the question naturally arises, what use is all this head scratching, this cogitating and struggle? How does this help kids develop career skills and practical adult knowledge? Well, one question I would ask back is how has the *absence* of many of these philosophical inquiries contributed to a sane and flourishing adult world? How has the overriding focus on information technology, test-taking, and even STEM disciplines—science, technology, engineering, and mathematics—impacted our present lives? To what extent have they alleviated economic hardship; divisions among classes, cultures, and races; authoritarian governance; social isolation; rates of anxiety, depression, addiction, and violence? Are we so much better off because of the externalizing, materialistic, and mechanizing world we have thus far provided? Again, to hark back to the question of the need for critical thinking and reflection on premises, I would have to answer both yes and no. Yes to the extent that there have been doubtless improvements to the general standard of living for most U.S. citizens since the pre-industrial eras of the 17th and 18th centuries. We have greater access to food, medicine, shelter, and communications than ever before. Our transportation and manufacturing sectors are much more efficient. But the ever-growing "worm in the ointment" is how bereft we are of enlivening moral directions, and of the workings of our inner worlds and capacities to cultivate those worlds. How bereft we are of that vibrant center I speak of—the capacity for presence, openness, and discernment[6]—and, in contrast, how filled we've become with fleeting attention spans, hollow relationships, and entrancements with machines. And I haven't even mentioned how dangerous this way of living has become through our desperation for quick fixes and instant answers, strong-arm leaders, and simplified slogans. The problem is that too many of us are not centered; we're extreme, fanatical, closed up.

So the question of bringing critical inquiry to our educational system is not a Left Wing plot; it's not an attempt to sway kids one way or another. It's an attempt to help kids think substantively on their own and open them to what really matters about their lives (alongside of and potentially beyond what their parents taught them and that may benefit society as a whole). It's an effort to bring wholeness and balance to an educational system that has faltered notably when it comes to fostering inner lives and discerning values; and that has too readily given in to profit-driven powers that have used the system for their own corporate ends—whether commercial or political (but rarely societal and ethical).

What is the Take-Home Message?

So what would this new educational system—and its centered approach—look like in the world? This is, of course, not a simple question, and I have no clear blueprint for the answer. However, I do think some outlines of an answer are evident (see also Heterodox Academy's website for an elaboration).[7] First, I think it would help many more people to pause and deliberate before reflexively acting, especially in morally ambiguous situations. This would likely mean that people and daily life would slow down to an extent, become more attentive, and be more open to creative ways of thinking and acting with one another. It would also likely mean that people will be more "care-ful" with one another and how they treat the natural world. If you are centered in the many ways of perceiving others and the world, then it is probable that you will consider hurtful and potentially harmful sides of your deliberations as well as joyful and potentially constructive sides, and that this tussling will accentuate care. It is also probable that you will consider the consequences of your actions, which will constrain reckless whims or impulses. The net effect then is likely to be an enlivening mix of openness and conscientiousness, spontaneity and discipline. You will have a greater capacity to get a sense of the larger context of a situation—for example, the emotional fragility of the person you're interacting with as well as the concrete demands (e.g., time or resources) of the moment.

Being comparatively centered will not bring paradise. It will not resolve illnesses, fears, or death. But it is likely to bring many more options to life's challenges, along with the strength and skillset to decide on those options, and to adapt to changing conditions. Thus, wouldn't it be better for the majority of people (and I mean diverse people on this planet) to prize both individuality and communalism; material comfort and emotional fulfillment; practical activity and spiritual connection; vital productivity and restful surrender, acceptance of what is; social support and individual initiative; standards of safety and openness, autonomy? The question, of course, is how such polarities are reconciled and managed. At what point is one or another polarity emphasized, sacrificed? Again, no easy answer, but if kids are immersed in questions like these from their earliest years (as appropriate) to the later stages of their development, my sense is that they will have had much practice working with and finding suitable ways to address life's contrasts and contradictions. At the least, they will have physical and emotional tools to work with such difficulties, whereas in the absence of those tools we see the results daily—broken homes and communities.

Another example of how these difficulties can be worked with in real life is illustrated by the energizing compromises that result from effective psychotherapy and mentoring. There are numerous examples of people finding ways to maintain ties with previously problematic or even abusive relatives following successful therapy. These people draw clear boundaries with those relatives (that they had not been able to do in the past) and yet find a degree of fulfillment in their closely monitored, limited contact with them. Mentoring and life coaching have also produced such outcomes. Or we can see a similar result in people who have been supported to maintain their autonomy for a creative project or life philosophy while also finding great and fulfilling intimacy with a romantic partner, whereas in pre-therapeutic or mentoring times they may not even have entertained such a dynamic situation. Such people recognize, in other words, that you don't have to "throw the baby out with the bathwater" and that vital aspects of life can be salvaged even in the face of other aspects being sacrificed. This is the creative challenge for most of us on this planet, let alone for the education of our children.

A course in philosophy then is one critical step in helping children find the balance points that can lead to richer and more fulfilled lives. But we shouldn't stop there. We need much more immersion in the Arts and Humanities from a variety of cultures to find out how people have handled their anxieties throughout the ages.[8] We also need these courses to counterbalance the trend toward technical and vocational education that is necessary for many to make a living but do not generally raise questions about *how* one will approach that living, or even why a given career is a priority for them. Courses in the Arts and Humanities (including the visual arts, literature, history, comparative religions, cultural anthropology, psychology, sociology, and philosophy, as previously mentioned) are essential in helping students home in on what really matters about their own life-paths as well as the life-paths of many on our planet. Studies of symbols, myths, rituals, historical cycles, religious and spiritual perspectives, cultural values, and socioeconomic systems, along with ways to think critically about them, add immeasurably to the quest for desirable jobs and how best to engage those jobs.[9]

At the foundation of this vibrantly centered education is what I call "emotionally restorative relationships." These are relationships in which people feel heard and seen and that get at the roots of their problems. They are also relationships that restore the sense of wonder and discovery that so often get buried in the work-a-day haste of deadlines, budgetary priorities, and the emphasis on technology. You might ask what are we "restoring"? We're restoring that primal sense of aliveness that I propose we all feel at the point of our arrival in life. It is the point of wholeness in the sense that we are deeply in touch with our vulnerability as well as connection to and amazement at the world. It is also the humanity we all share, *prior* to our familial, cultural, and tribal identities and thereby traumas and constraints of those identities as well. But we are not exempted from the primal trauma of being born; we all share that wound. It's just that birth trauma is quickly followed by birth drama, the wonder and amazement of being alive, the combination that forms our vibrant center.

To the extent we are restored, therefore, it is toward our unbridled wholeness and our original aliveness, which encompasses *both* our vulnerable and venturesome natures.

It can't be overstated that whatever familial and cultural identifications we must grapple with, particularly if we are an oppressed minority, it is equally important to do one's best to address the seed of those tensions. Like all major tensions we experience as developing human beings, we must get at the primal root if we are to substantively promote individual and collective well-being. This means that we must address the helplessness and groundlessness of our emergence into life and the potential for transforming that fragility through emotionally restorative relationships. Emotionally restorative relationships not only enlarge our capacity for wonder, but eventually through consistent contact, support us to convert that wonder into greater presence, openness, and discernment, the critical ingredients for a vibrantly centered life.

It is also increasingly clear that emotionally restorative relationships are needed globally to address the emotionally impoverished relationships that pervade almost every major sector of our lives. These sectors include parenting, education, business and finance, medicine, politics and consumerism, and even aspects of religious, spiritual, and psychological services. The increasing reliance on cell phones, media silos, streaming platforms, chat-bots, education and therapy bots, and the AI-mediated world in general are major deviation points from our native capacity to cultivate presence, openness, and discernment. They are also limiting kids from being exposed to resources that embody presence, openness, and discernment, thus limiting them from even knowing what they may be missing in the absence of those qualities. Where are the teachers who have the time and support to raise core questions about values, ethics, and truth? Where are the parents who can throw their hand-held devices aside and focus on key conversations about books, movies, school assignments, and matters of deep personal significance with their kids? Where are the doctors who can afford to slide away from their laptops and provide concerted, face-to-face discussions about their patients' questions, concerns, and personal health goals? Where are businesspeople who can take the time to explore moral and ethical aspects of their production lines or profit margins? Where are the politicians and diplomats who are willing to engage in honest, person-to-person dialogues with those on the "other side," or with the public they serve? Where are the clergy who co-create an atmosphere of inquiry and candid discussion about the nature and relevance of doctrine to the current struggles of congregants' lives? All too diminishing, in my estimation.

The aim of vibrant centering in education needs to prepare children for this increasingly polarized world. It needs to vividly bring to their attention the alternatives to emotionally impoverished relationships, jobs, and cultures. Among these alternatives are emotionally restorative relationships that, hopefully, will help them to become the workers, teachers, spiritual and social leaders of a rejuvenated era—an era that uses machines for humane purposes and that contributes to the meaning and awe that can reinvigorate human life. Now that so many in our post-industrial world have so few absolutes to draw upon, so few traditional authorities, it is imperative that students develop their own (inner) authorities. These inner authorities or centers will then prepare students to sift through the emerging deluge—cultural, political, and technological—that is about to inundate their lives and assist them to make the best of that deluge, to separate the "wheat from the chaff."

We now turn to the area of work and how vibrantly centered, emotionally restorative relationships can help to create an entirely fresh vocational life. This is a life that combines practical financial aims with intimate needs for meaning and a sense of participation in the rich and vast possibilities beyond one's own isolated domain.

Chapter 3

The Vibrant Center of Work

Not that it was ever a panacea, but the American business model has taken major hits in recent times. The rise of privatization in the place of government-supported healthcare, public education, international distribution of food, gun regulations, environmental protections, food and drug protections, monetary and credit protections, artistic and academic freedoms, science, and public broadcasting have all but subsumed our current way of life. The so-called "art of the deal," which too often translates into "quid pro quo," transactional relationships with formerly morally minded or at least morally inclined institutions such as state governments, legal authorities, universities, schools, libraries, and museums are also permeating our society. Moreover, some of these transactions have the flavor of mob-like extortionist tactics, where if your agency or business does not comply, it will suffer physical or personal harm.

Is this polarized mentality what we really want to see in our republic, in our day-to-day relations with one another?

Making Work Meaningful

From a vibrant center point of view, our first question about work must be: How do we provide maximal training for maximal vocational meaning at a manageable cost? These are the kinds of "paradoxes" that organizational experts such as Wendy K. Smith and Marianne W. Lewis have been informing businesses how to navigate for decades. Their research indicates that the best business leaders and workers adopt a "both/and" rather than "either/or" mindset, and that they *engage* tensions, such as those between local community traditions and economic needs, organizational intimacy and expanding corporate size, attunement to moral issues and needs for profit. The researchers assert that the best organizational leaders model both/and approaches in their oversight of their organizations as well as in their treatment of employees. As the researchers elaborate:

> Outfitted with the tools of both/and thinking, these leaders "seek out underlying paradoxes to address them head-on and...generate solutions that are more creative and sustainable. Doing so moves [them] into the *engaging zone*—where [they] both experience tensions and adopt a paradox mindset.
>
> In our research, we explored how these zones impact people at work. We found that the people in the engaging zone performed better at work. They were seen as more innovative and productive by their managers, [and] not only that, but they were also more satisfied with their jobs.[1]

While the vibrantly centered education discussed above is assuredly foundational for such a paradoxical mindset—as well as a meaningful and affordable career path—what might that path and mindset actually look like? What are they beginning to look like now? For one thing, those qualities are improving workers' motivation. By this I mean that vibrantly centered work is increasingly choiceful work. It's enabling workers to explore an expanding range of options. Thus, instead of being a passive recipient to powers that be, the emerging workforce is becoming a stakeholder in their company. Increasingly, they have a meaningful say in how the company conducts business, what goods it produces, and what impact the company has on the community it serves.

This emerging model may also someday provide a "well-being forum;" regular employee meetings that encourage active listening and discussion of topics directly relevant to what brings workers alive in their work tasks, what deeply matters about their jobs, and how they can improve them. What follows shows how the meetings might work. First, they would be voluntary and confidential—meaning that a boss or fellow employee would be prohibited from using any disclosure in the meeting as a pretext for any work-related action (short of a threat to harm self or others, of course). Second, and as a reinforcement for the latter, workers would be encouraged to have one-on-one sessions with coaches or consultants prior to group meetings to resolve personal issues with work.[2] The group meetings, on the other hand. would emphasize topics of collective interest (e.g., job satisfaction, meaning, or community implications) rather than the particular concerns of single individuals. This does not mean that single individuals would be prohibited from bringing up personal concerns but that the framing of the discussion would be around whatever is brought up as a group concern, thus limiting personal disclosure and risk. In total, such well-being forums would provide a concerted opportunity for employees to discuss the implications of their work for themselves, their families, and the communities they serve. The meetings could also feature workshops from time to time on mental and physical health, as well as organizational well-being, financial solvency, and any of a range of topics that are relevant to workers' jobs and lives. As indicated, organizational and mental health consultants would be hired on a stand-by basis to provide optimal support for workers' personal and collective concerns. Who would pay for such an addition to work culture? Ideally, employers would pay, not only because it would likely benefit their bottom line—as well as worker motivation, attrition, and productivity—but also because an atmosphere of presence, openness, and discernment would become the new imperative value. Of course, other sources of funding would be needed in the case of employers with limited financial means. But this is where vibrant-center reforms should lead to governmental and philanthropic alternatives and the question of whether we (the taxpayer, the donor) prioritize a gratified and inspired workforce as much if not more than one that turns out products at increasing costs of alienation, stress, isolation, addiction, and bitterness—which couldn't be helpful for any bottom line either qualitatively or quantitatively.

These recommendations are highly resonant with the approach discussed above, as well as a major 2025 survey of employees' concerns about work. This is what the survey of 2,017 employees concluded:

> The well-being of the workforce remains paramount, with a strong desire among employees for organizations that genuinely value their mental and emotional health. However, the data signals a potential complacency in providing easily accessible mental health resources—a trend that could undermine employee well-being, particularly for those working in manual labor or customer-facing roles.
>
> A key takeaway from this year's survey is that working in one's preferred environment can have a profound impact on workers. The survey data indicates that neither in-person nor remote nor hybrid work is an inherently better way to work. Rather, workers may see psychological benefits such as higher job satisfaction, improved mental health, and a stronger sense of purpose when their individual preferences and work arrangements align. Such findings suggest a crucial shift in organizational thinking: rather than dictating a singular "best" work model, the survey suggests that employers should strive for flexibility and personalization to optimize employee well-being and productivity.

Recommendations

In 2025, the imperative for employers in the United States that seek to improve psychological well-being in the workplace is clear: to move beyond simply reacting to change and instead proactively cultivate work environments that prioritize well-being, embrace flexibility, champion inclusivity, and foster genuine alignment between leadership and the workforce. By addressing these aims, organizations not only can navigate the current era of transformation but also unlock the full potential of their human capital, creating a more fulfilling and productive future for all workers in America.[3]

Emotionally Restorative Relationships as Pillars of Work Culture

In sum, a vibrantly centered worksite fosters *emotionally restorative relationships*. These are relationships in which workers feel heard and seen and that, to the degree appropriate to their work context, get at the roots of their concerns. To be clear, I am not talking about some "pie in the sky" ideal here, but a practical, holistic approach that enhances workers' motivations, engagement with their jobs, and feeling of participation in a larger cause of family, community, and life on our planet. I am also talking about an approach that is supported by strong evidence as exemplified by Smith and Lewis's "both/and" approach to organizational health, as well as the 2025 survey of employees concerns cited above. To be sure, it will take significant funding and resources to create such work communities, but, again, this addition is implicit in a new, vibrantly centered mentality. If we really think through what is needed at all these levels of living—from parenting to education to work—we need to equally reflect on how such a society can support these reforms. This inquiry takes us to the economic and governmental underpinnings of a new consciousness, which we will discuss in a later chapter.

Circling back to the vibrant center of work as well as parenting and education, we can now see how necessary emotionally restorative relationships are to address the emotionally impoverished relationships that are devastating our communities. In addition to the proposals I outlined above, I believe the Experiential Democracy Dialogue (or something like it) will play a central role in the dismantling of emotionally impoverished relationships at work. This dialogue format would provide consistent opportunities for workers (or workers and managers) to engage in safe (e.g., structured, confidential), supportive dialogues when conflicts arise. It would especially be of help when issues of race, religion, and class emerge, as these are some of the thorniest problems in workplace relations. Integrating psychologically trained facilitators, as previously noted, would be a chief priority in this vision of a more vibrant, holistic work setting. I can see the great value of having such facilitators on standby or even in regular touch with day-to-day workers, supporting them to work out personal issues that arise during work hours as well as interpersonal tensions. This would no longer be a "top-down" organizational structure or, as the study above noted, a singular "best" work model for employees, which I witnessed aplenty during a stint with a large financial company; rather, it would be a model that attunes much more to individual preferences and concerns.

The Role of AI

It is also imperative, as the study above suggests, that we look very carefully at the changing nature of work due to AI and the information economy. As workers noted in the survey, AI and enhanced technology can improve their work output and effectiveness, but it also can disparage and replace them. This problem was especially evident for frontline workers who are more susceptible to monotonous routines or even replacement than managerial or upper level employees. In addition to co-ownership, there needs to be a way to provide frontline workers with more of a sense of agency, creativity, and control over their work operations than they currently enjoy. This is where group meetings, bridge-building dialogues, and individual counseling could also be invaluable toward enhancing workers' plight.

As AI increasingly takes over our work lives, it begs the question of how we will find meaning in the absence of such traditional engagements. What will we do, how will we be when there is less structure in our day and when more and more of our needs are filled by mechanized beings? The vibrant center of consciousness is instructive here as well because it enables us to think "outside the box" but also realistically about how we might live. It could, in fact, be a marvelous opportunity to tap into resources we never thought of or had the time for before, such as the creation of a work of art, the crafting of items that bring pleasure to households, children, and communities. Taking up a musical instrument or singing could become a much more pervasive pursuit, and universities could become hotbeds of continuing education for many.

But perhaps most important, the degree to which we can use our devices to give us substantive and lasting pleasure will be key. There is a wide and deep world of possibility out there for encouragement of conversations, for creative use of chat and video platforms to create engaging stories, musical performances, plays, and bedtime reading for children. The devices could also be used to explore the broader worlds of science, religion, philosophy, the arts, and entertainment. They will open doors for travel and discovery, and not just virtually but in actuality as they improve our systems of transportation. They could also be put to work to help solve our problems with climate change, energy needs, and preservation of the environment, not to mention some of our most vexing medical challenges. The point, again, is that we need to oversee and direct the new technology, and we need to bring our creative input into their calculations and productions. This human-centered mastery of machines could create an entire industry of consultants, specialists, and designers in itself.

Chapter 4

The Vibrant Center of Religion and Spirituality

I begin here with an allegory that illustrates both the perils and possibilities in contemporary religion. Consider this quote from the highly acclaimed British film *Conclave* (2024):[1]

> Certainty.
> Certainty is the great enemy of unity.
> Certainty is the deadly enemy of tolerance.
> Even Christ was not certain at the end.
> My God, My God, why have you forsaken me?
> He cried out in his agony at the ninth hour on the cross.
> Our faith is a living thing,
> precisely because it walks hand-in-hand with doubt.
> If there was only certainty...
> and no doubt...
> there would be no mystery...
> and therefore no need... for faith.
> Let us pray that God will grant us a Pope who doubts.
> And let [that God] grant us a Pope who sins and asks for forgiveness,
> and who carries on.
>
> ~ Cardinal Lawrence, Manager of the Conclave

On the face of it, *Conclave* is about a bunch of middle-aged men sitting around and deciding on a new pope to replace the old one who just died. But to my mind, this cinematically masterful, philosophically trailblazing film is about much more than a gathering of staid old guys upholding the fundaments of Catholic tradition. It is about us, our world today, and the *carelessness* with which it is increasingly treated. I'm reminded here of Nick Carraway's comment in F. Scott Fitzgerald's 1925 novel *The Great Gatsby* about the "careless" people around Gatsby's ex-lover Daisy.[2] It is an all too contemporary observation.

Coupling Conviction with Doubt: The New Challenge of Religiosity

As with the film, our world today is splintered by three basic, foundation-shaking problems: abject absolutism, amoral relativism, and agonizing (often agnostic) struggles between them that *potentially* can lead to a new communal consciousness, a vibrantly centered consciousness that both recognizes and makes the best of our paradoxical state. This would be a state where human beings are both vulnerable, rule-bound creatures *and* courageous adventure-seeking explorers.

In the movie, these positions were brought to life by the dynamics of the Conclave, that decision-making body of Cardinals assembled at the Sistine Chapel in Rome. The main protagonists are vying to become the next Pope at the Conclave. You have the absolute and rule-bound orientation of the Roman Cardinal Tedesco; the ostensibly liberal yet expedient and amoral relativist (to the extent such a conservative institution allows) Cardinal Tremblay, who like some unmoored libertarians and free-market capitalists today will do anything to gain power or make a buck; and then you have the more performatively liberal but limitedly discerning Cardinal Bellini, who eventually—and naively—embraces Cardinal Tremblay (to avoid the installment of the dogmatist Tedesco); and finally you have Cardinal Lawrence, who strives mightily to confront the moral ambiguities of both the liberal and conservative factions and who gives a speech (partly quoted at the top of this article) about the dangers of certitude Left or Right that is worthy of a Paul Tillich stemwinder.[3] This speech also captivates Sister Agnes, the rather disparaged nun among the group who gradually joins Cardinal Lawrence in grappling with the extremist positions exemplified by the other cardinals. In the film's crescendo, you have Cardinal Benitez, the priest from Kabul of all places(!), who wrestles with the extremes—both literally and figuratively—with his whole bodily being (which includes his deeply personal tussling with having a rare yet ironically timely condition of possessing a female uterus). In other words, Cardinal Benitez is a hermaphrodite.

The distinguishing factor regarding the latter three clerics, it seems to me, is their embodiment of presence, whereas the other characters appear driven much more by insecurity and fear, some of which is justified following a series of terrorist bombings by Islamicists just outside the Sistine Chapel. Still, it is the Kabul priest Benitez in particular who upsets the apple cart in so many ways by expressing a discerning yet flexible center that acknowledges crimes of both past and present but also hints at a more discovery oriented, attuned future: that is, a future that acknowledges our need to stem the chaos of the world but also holds out a hand to foster dialogue and creative coexistence. Here's his speech following a diatribe against relativism by Cardinal Tedesco in reaction to the terrorist bombing outside the Chapel walls. Remarkably and, to my mind, fortuitously, this speech by Benitez won over the Conclave of stodgy old guys who seemed to intuit deep down that something radical had to shift in order for not only religion (or in its highest expression, morality) but also our world to survive. First, I quote Cardinal Tedesco's outburst for context:

> Here at last we see the result of the
> doctrine of relativism

> so beloved by our liberal brothers!
> A relativism that sees all faiths and passing fancies accorded equal weight.
> So that now, when we look around us, we see the homeland
> of the Holy Roman Catholic Church
> dotted with the mosques and minarets
> of the prophet Muhammad!
> You should be ashamed, ashamed...
> We should all be ashamed!
> We tolerate Islam in our land,
> but they revile us in theirs.
> We nourish them in our homelands.
> But they exterminate us.
> How long will we persist in this weakness?
> They are literally at our walls right now.
> What we need now is a leader who understands
> that we are facing a true religious war…
> Yes, a religious war.
> We need a leader who will put a stop to the drift
> that has gone on almost ceaselessly for the past 50 years.
> How long will we have to persist in this weakness,
> how long?
> We need a leader…who fights these animals![4]

Here is Cardinal Benitez's reply:

> Is this the man you want to lead us?
> My brother Cardinal…
> With respect.
> What do you know about war?
> I carried out my ministry in the Congo.
> In Baghdad, in Kabul.
> I've seen the lines of the dead and wounded,
> Christian and Muslim.

Would you say we have to fight?
What is it you think we're fighting?
Do you think it's those deluded men
who had carried out these terrible acts today?
No, my brother.
The thing you're fighting is here… inside each
and every one of us if we give in to hate now,
[that is] if we speak of "sides" instead of speaking for
    every man and woman.
This is my first time here, amongst you,
and I suppose it will be my last.
Forgive me, but these last few days we have shown
ourselves to be small petty men, we have seemed
concerned only with ourselves,
with Rome, with these elections, with power.
But things are not the Church.
The Church is not tradition.
The Church is not the past.
The Church is what we do next.[5]

Toward a Vibrant Center of Religiosity

Now it is clear to me, and what Cardinal Benitez makes plain in his speech, is that symbolically speaking, not only the church today but our world has got to deal with males born with wombs. We have got to deal with that which is other, foreign, and different—whether that's the recently decolonized, the ethnically and racially marginalized, the politically disenfranchised, the gender and sexually dehumanized, or even the technologically synthesized whose forms would hardly be imaginable just a few short years ago.

Are we even clear about what it means to be a human being in these times? Are we prepared for the varieties of humanity that are emerging? Do we not need a much more nimble and flexible psyche to work with these colliding realities, lest we bury our heads in the sand with authoritarian rules to stave off the inevitable complexity of our future and ironically foster much worse chaos, much more destruction that such polarized minds have purported to suppress?

The upshot is that we need and will need more deliberative and consoling souls like cardinals Lawrence and Benitez—as well as Sister Agnes. We'll need folks who recognize *both* that we're moving too fast with our cultural and technological changes and that we risk fascistic and authoritarian breakdown to put the brakes on these changes. We need people who express more of a *vibrant center*, who can deeply and thoughtfully provide moral compasses for us and yet at the same time recognize when these compasses are outdated and in need of revision.

In short, we need to cultivate greater *presence* in the world today—that is, the holding and illuminating of that which is palpably significant within and between people. This presence could then foster a more fluid, flexible, yet also discerning populace, a populace that develops what I call *life-enhancing anxiety.* This is the capacity to live with and make the best of the depth and mystery of existence or, more concretely, the capacity to live much more on the edge of wonder and discovery as distinct from terror and overwhelm—the reverse of so many mentalities today.[6]

So how do we move in this present-centered direction, the direction of life-enhancing anxiety? The great American literary scholar Ralph Waldo Emerson gives us a hint when he wrote that "Jove nods to Jove behind each of us."[7] A little background: "Jove" is conventionally used as a poetic reference to the god Jupiter from Roman mythology. But I think Emerson meant it here in the more symbolic sense, as the "sacred realm" that in some sense reflects our universal *connection* not only to each other but to the cosmos, creation itself, out of which we all emerged. Is this not what we experience when we feel maximally present with ourselves and others? Is this not that awesome and, I propose, cross-cultural sense that we are being deeply *met* and deeply moved?

It is a form of intimacy to be sure, but it is *ontological* intimacy, not only intimacy between people.

This realm of the sacred or being cosmically *met* may be the most important dimension to salvage as we humans plunge into this disjointed era of quick fixes and fragmentary values. By "cosmically met" I harken to Tillich's concept of "Listening Love" and Buber's notion of "I–Thou."[8] The greater the presence or attention we pay to a given encounter the more it has a cosmic significance, a cosmological scope, as distinct from the restrictive and fetishized scope of a knee-jerk reaction, or a pre-set doctrine. It's the immersion in all possible sides of a given encounter—the good, the bad, and the ugly; mind, body, and spirit—that gives us the best chance at a humane and discerning response.

We have so much outer estrangement today in the form of wars, violence, and political and cultural divisiveness precisely because we fail to address the inner estrangement that precedes it. As noted in a previous chapter, I call this inner estrangement the *"polarized mind."* The polarized mind is the fixation on a single point of view to the utter exclusion of competing points of view and can apply to anarchic relativism as well as dogmatic absolutism, wherever one is desperately clinging or unclinging.[9]

This disquieting range of the polarized mind is due to its basis in fear, particularly the primal fear of difference or that which is other, which leads to a sense of *helplessness and groundlessness.* In turn, this sense of helplessness and groundlessness, in the absence of inner work, links to all kinds of destructive extremes, as I have intimated earlier in the book. Among these are cultural and political dehumanization. But also, and not least, religious criminality and fanaticism.

This then is no time to "rearrange deck chairs on the Titanic." To stem the vicious "tit for tat" cycle of polarization we urgently need to prioritize what Tillich prophetically called the depth dimension.[10] This is a dimension in which our inner lives are taken as seriously as those that heretofore have been outward facing, materialistic, and symptom based.

It is in this light that our religious and spiritual institutions are called to lead from a vibrant center. They need to preach presence, openness, and discernment, which is, in fact, the best of what many great religious and spiritual traditions prioritize. Consider embracing the stranger, showing mercy, spreading compassion, empowering the disenfranchised, resisting the oppressor, and alerting us to the awesomeness of life. Assuredly, religions and spiritual leaders are well aware of these foundational teachings. But too often the teachings become obscured by doctrinal dogmas, ceremonial routines, or appeasements to clay-footed authorities. Where, for example, are our religious leaders on the issues of gun violence, climate change, and polarizing political figures? Why not underscore more of the values we share in common as human beings, not just sectarian congregants—values such as the need for safety, dignity, community, and a deep veneration for life? And then invite human beings of all life-affirming denominations to participate in dialogues together as to how to concretely address our shared needs.[11]

Indeed, religious and spiritual institutions could and should play a larger role supporting but also reflecting critically on cross-culturally shared values. These are values that have been established in the psychological literature in studies worldwide. Among these shared values (or moral beliefs) are: first, the concern with *harm and care* or "prioritizing care for vulnerable people or animals, reducing suffering, eschewing cruelty"; second, fostering *fairness and reciprocity* or the promotion of "equality, the elimination of cheating," and "having proportionality of outcomes"; third, prioritizing the *ingroup and loyalty* or "patriotism, self-sacrifice for the group, nonbetrayal"; fourth, stressing *authority and respect* or "valuing obedience, following leadership, respecting hierarchies"; and fifth, underscoring *purity and sanctity* or "preventing bodily contamination," enhancing "dietary and sexual practices," and promoting "hygiene and cleanliness."[12] To the extent that clergy and spiritual teachers draw on a vibrant center of consciousness (and conscientiousness), they are key to helping multicultural populations find their own vibrant centers along the spectrum of the above-shared beliefs. Questions such as What does prioritizing care for vulnerable people, animals, and ecosystems look like? How does one reduce suffering and stem cruelty? How does a group promote equality? To what extent is patriotism and self-sacrifice for the group ethically sound? What does valuing obedience mean in daily life or, for that matter, respecting hierarchies and prioritizing purity and sanctity?—these are all extremely relevant inquiries for today's religious and spiritual leadership.

I would also venture to propose that the sense of awe toward life is a shared human value, perhaps a core value. By this I mean that the humility and wonder or sense of adventure toward living begins at birth and blossoms into both a sober appreciation of the vastness of existence as well as a lively fascination with the mystery of existence. So many of our morals, rituals, and forms of worship or adoration are premised on this sense of the preciousness and amazement of human life. Just think of the impact our religious and spiritual leaders could have on our society and world if they conveyed the richness of these dimensions and integrated them more explicitly into sermons, rituals, and conceptions of God or Spirit. Just think about how much more invigorating their teachings would be if such leaders parted from their sectarian dogmas and reached people at these very human levels.

One way to achieve this integration is to provide periodic opportunities for leaders from diverse religious and spiritual traditions to speak in one's own house of worship. Thus, Buddhists, Christians, Jews, Muslims, Hindus, Taoists could be invited alone or in various combinations to speak and perform rituals in one another's places of worship. That way, each formerly staid tradition could begin to learn about the others, experience their connection with creation, taste their food, witness their style of dress, observe (or participate in!) their rituals, and so on. Such mixing does not at all mean that each religious or spiritual group needs to lose its own essential identities, but it does mean that those identities may expand and embrace the deeper humanity we all share. For, after all, is this not what the prominent religions are all about, deepening and enlarging our sense of cosmic connection, elevating the state of *all* humanity? Isn't this the essence of living religions, religions that evolve as human beings evolve, and as human understanding evolves? To be sure, there are religious and spiritual traditions that are already engaging in this kind of structured openness. I have witnessed them myself in certain reconstructionist versions of Judaism and ecumenical versions of Christianity, Islamism, Hinduism, Buddhism, and Taoism. But they are few and far between. If we are to move toward a vibrantly centered world, a coexisting and sustainable world, we need to significantly accelerate that interfaith—and "interbeing"—dimension, as the great Buddhist teacher Thich Nhat Hanh put it. I will discuss Thich Nhat Hanh at greater length in Chapter 7.

Finally, there needs to be a place for the spiritually searching population that does not wish to participate in religious ritual per se but that deeply values connection with our cosmic surround. These are people who have been called "Nones" or nonreligiously aligned but often spiritually seeking individuals.[13] I consider myself one of those people, although I have strong familial and cultural ties to Judaism, particularly the Judaism of Buber, Heschel, and Spinoza. Yet I also feel a strong connection with a range of nondogmatic, philosophical and spiritually oriented groups. For me this "enchanted agnosticism" is an awe-based sensibility that opens to the thrill and the anxiety, humility and wonder of everyday experience and sometimes includes religious ritual, especially of the preverbal, embodied kind, such as choral singing and music. To me, this communal experience of the Beyond is the essence of religiosity and the miraculous in life. But I also experience such vibrance when walking in nature, swimming in the ocean, communing with loved ones, and witnessing great cities, films, books, cross-cultural and cross-disciplinary conversations, or focused in depth conversations. I also experience this vibrance with night skies and nonhuman animals, museums and creative architecture, fresh air and good health. Enchanted agnosticism takes mystery seriously and affirms the miracle of life seriously. It takes me to the "multitude" of selves that Whitman speaks of as well as the inquiry and clarity that both art and science yield.[14] Will enchanted agnosticism or some form of it become more prevalent in the future? I hope so, as I believe it captures core aspirations in each of the prominent religions—and sciences.

Now we turn to perhaps the central influence of our lives today—ideology and government. How do we proceed with a vibrant center of both societal philosophy and legislative follow-through, collective governance? This is the encompassing inquiry I now put before us.

Chapter 5

The Vibrant Center in Government

Let me be clear. I'm no policy expert or constitutional scholar. The following is not a detailed plan for government reform. That said, I do have experience with organizational leadership and the facilitation of psychologically and spiritually enriched lives. That is what this book is about. In that light, the following is a framework that I believe could greatly enhance governance. It is a framework of psychospiritual[1] *processes* that could, if thoughtfully implemented, contribute to the ethical and spiritual soundness of governance as a whole. And it begins with presence, openness, and discernment.

Because it prizes diverse perspectives, dialogue, and discernment, a vibrant-centered government could also go a long way toward unifying populations in the United States and beyond that are currently fragmented, resentful, and even rageful toward one another. Vibrant-centered governance will not unify in the sense of forced conformity but in the light of appreciative inquiry, discovery, and the potential for expanding common ground. It will strive for that prophetic and timely call by 19th century poet Samuel Taylor Coleridge for "multeity in unity."[2] This is Coleridge's trope for a messy yet convivial life-path.

Are there examples of such presence, openness, and discernment (the vibrant center) in governance today? Yes. It seems to me that they are evident wherever a governing body has carefully weighed and addressed the paradoxes of life. One historical example with continued relevance is the paradox of George Washington. His well-known decision to limit himself to two terms in office when he had every opportunity to become a virtual king is "Exhibit A" of this paradox. That this humbling act has, with perhaps a handful of egregious exceptions, distinguished U.S. presidents from kings for over two centuries is another example of its significance. Another enduring paradox is that of the U.S. Constitution which holds that three co-equal branches of government—the judiciary, the executive, and the legislative—serve as checks and balances over one another's sovereign power. And still another is the Constitutional separation of powers, such that religion can be practiced privately but not as an official ideology of the government. Of course, there have been many reckless paradoxes throughout our country's history as well, such as the sanctioning of slavery or the wanton destruction of Native Americans in an otherwise "democratic" society. But because these paradoxes did not come anywhere close to being vibrantly centered—that is care-fully weighed and addressed—they were not only reckless but appallingly destructive.

Another much later example of carefully weighing and addressing paradox was the virtually unprecedented decision to aid Germany after World War II. The Marshall Plan, for instance, provided millions of dollars in aid to a decimated populace to incentivize them to develop a freer, more diversified society that in the long run could contribute to a more peaceful and stabilized world. The Marshall Plan is a particularly valuable example of a vibrantly centered federal policy because it meant that the victors of a very costly world conflict were able to tolerate the idea of providing aid and comfort to a formerly vicious adversary in the service of a higher goal of world peace. Moreover, the Marshall Plan worked—effectively persuading Germany to take a democratic path, with much greater consciousness of its destructive past. This outcome, of course, stood in sharp contrast to the Treaty at Versailles after World War I. That so-called treaty, like so many in history, was both lopsided and vengeful, handing almost all the spoils to the victors and virtually none to those they defeated. Instead of holding the paradox of the need for accountability for that war on the one hand, while extending a hand of support for long-term reconstruction and transformation, on the other, the formulators of the Versailles Treaty came straight at their German captors with punishing economic demands. This action led in turn to one of the most devastating economic collapses in history; and it was that collapse that led significantly to the eventual rise of both Hitler and the fascist state.[3]

Let me be clear that I am not advocating for some kind of complacent moderation here. There is a place for moderation, of course, but some moderates, such as Camus, as we shall see later, also recognize that to be genuinely centered is to sometimes think outside the box, whereas compulsive moderation can also enable a corrupt status quo. How many moderates, for example, have enabled dictatorial political leaders to amplify their power? Our focus should be on deeply intentional action, not on keeping things calm, balanced, or routine but on what needs to be done at any given moment. Each of the examples I provide above are illustrations of people and institutions that "heeded the demand of the hour," to paraphrase the philosopher Martin Buber.[4] Or to put it more concretely, they made decisions on the basis of deep deliberation and concerted agency.

An Office of Psychological Advisors

It is in this light that I propose an Office of Psychological Advisors (or OPA), roughly on a par with the active military, to occupy a central place in our government.[5] I know this may sound outlandish, improbable to achieve. But I don't think I'm alone in declaring that such an arm of government is now at least as urgent if not more so than the vast operations to both instigate and defend ourselves against war. To put it another way, why should we *not* prioritize an arm of government that bolsters the mentality of our nation? The mentality of our nation (and all nations) is critical not only to the well-being of the populace but to actually preventing the kind of physical conflicts that lead to mass and individual violence in the first place! Why should we not have an office that supports and oversees the psychospiritual well-being of the populace just as much as a Department of Defense (now sadly called "Department of War") that supports and oversees the tragic consequences of rivaling parties incapable of finding humane means of resolving conflicts? It is high time in the evolution of our species for the establishment of a psychologically attuned, "live and let live" component of our day-to-day lives. And it is an imperative "next step" in the cultivation of a truly democratic society—a society that prizes the freedom and responsibility for our inner lives as much as it does the behavior and expression we've come to expect in the conduct of our outer lives. Such an evolution, in fact, is essential to the sustainment of the democratic functioning of our outer lives.

The OPA would ideally be established through an act of Congress, selected by a bipartisan congressional committee, and funded through taxation, just as our present military. It would also ideally draw on a much more equitable—that is, progressive—tax base, where those in the top income brackets would be responsible for commensurate contributions. In effect, they would be contributing to the psychospiritual well-being of the society that supports them, something akin to the social capitalism of Nordic countries that mix financial competitiveness with conscientiousness for the good of the collective. There could, of course, be a range of ways to fund such a new and critical arm of our government (including the thoughtful elimination of wasteful spending in the present government), and these should be pursued. But the social capitalist (sometimes called "social democratic") approach seems to me to be just as integral to vibrantly centered—present, open, and discerning—governance.

Once established, the OPA would comprise top-level professionals in psychology, psychiatry, social work, sociology, pastoral counseling, and other allied fields dedicated to one overarching task: the promotion of affordable and accessible emotionally restorative relationships across every major sector of society (including government itself). Again, emotionally restorative relationships epitomize the vibrant center. They are relationships where people feel heard and seen and that get at the roots of their problems. The mandate of this office would be ambitious to be sure, but, in my view, it is urgent to stem the emotionally impoverished relationships that are linked to just about every major social ill that our society now harbors. These ills include but are not limited to the high percentage of youth that are more bonded to their AI companions than their parents; the alarming rates of depression, anxiety, isolation, and addiction among both adults and children; the alarming rates of cultural and political divisions (echo chambers) that are leading to dehumanizing and sometimes lethal actions toward those who are considered different or foreign; the amplification of devaluing rhetoric from our cultural and political leaders; and the tendency toward authoritarian practices by political leaders. In my view, each of these problems has its basis in deficient human relations, as much or more than many of the other contexts conventionally attributed to them, such as genes, dietary and medical issues, availability of drugs and weaponry, propaganda. Again, if we don't help people address the underlying fears of their lives, frequently originating in impoverished relationships, then we have little chance of making vital and lasting changes in the society of which we are all a part.[6]

How then would an OPA actually proceed? First and foremost, it would support, fund, and incentivize helping professionals from all over the country to devote even a fraction of their week to providing affordable and accessible, emotionally restorative relationships in every major sector of our society. Among these sectors would be longer term, in-depth psychotherapy, particularly for underserved populations; mentoring and life-coaching for impoverished and marginalized youth; supportive, structured dialogues between culturally and politically diverse communities, and between culturally and politically diverse high school and college students; in-depth conflict mediation and facilitation of well-being groups in the work setting; nonsectarian spiritual and religious counseling for spiritual and religious seekers; and supportive, structured dialogues, such as the Experiential Democracy Dialogue and Braver Angels format for political and diplomatic leaders in conflict.

Given that *desperation* is a glaring and pervasive issue in our country, not only when it comes to mental health but also collective survival, it is equally imperative to have a more present-centered, open, and discerning legislative structure that addresses this desperation.

In this light, I propose either through an amendment to the U.S. Constitution, an act of Congress, or perhaps more realistically, as a voluntary pilot program, that the OPA also be tasked with delineating the psychospiritual processes that inform good governance. Let's call it a "pre-legislative protocol" or "protocol of civility." This protocol would begin with new criteria for political and diplomatic proceedings. The first criterion I propose is that in order to run for office, each congressional candidate and presidential candidate engage in at least one publicly accessible OPA-facilitated supportive, structured dialogue (such as the Experiential Democracy Dialogue) with a member of an opposing party who holds a contrasting view on a topic of mutual concern. Although this engagement would be mandatory in order to run for congressional and presidential offices, the visibility of the engagement—that is, the question of whether it can be transcribed or recorded—is a thornier issue. My own recommendation is that particularly for this pre-candidacy phase, the question of public access should be up to the participants in the dialogue. Those outcomes could be confined to descriptions of agreement and disagreement over specific policy issues. However, my sense is that there likely would be a "price to pay" for not allowing the public access to the entirety of the dialogue. I know as a voter that I would much rather see with my own eyes how a candidate comported themselves with their partner, both verbally and nonverbally. I'd also like to know how well each adhered to the ground rules and spoke from their hearts rather than spouted some phony talking points or party rhetoric. I'd also want to discover how much each partner can really "hear" the contrasting perspective of their adversarial partner and how fully each discloses both the personal and professional reasons they chose the positions they did. Finally, I would like to see how authentically each partner discusses what they learned about themselves, the other partner, and their relationship through the dialogue process. Could they approach each other with genuine curiosity and respect, if not for their respective opinions per se at least for the fact that they were willing to sit with and be vulnerable toward one another in some very personal exchanges. Finally, and naturally, I would want to know whether and to what extent each partner altered their opinions about their respective stances and perhaps even approached some common ground at points.

Now, it is no secret that candidates for political office tend to be good performers who could simply fake their way through all the phases of structured dialogue. But this dishonesty could also prove their undoing, particularly if they are observed by the public and particularly in light of the aim of these dialogue processes, which is to learn about and understand each other rather than "win" a debate or impose views on each other. If recorded, such a process would give the public a quite thorough sense of whether either partner is "mailing it in," performing for the crowd, or acting as a shill for powerful political or corporate interests. Perhaps more often than we realize, and particularly in an intimate setting like a mediated one-on-one dialogue, people can sniff out such pretenses or at the least have a clearer basis on which to judge the presence, openness, and discernment of the candidate's personal and professional style.

On the other hand, as noted, the partners could choose not to be recorded (except for the mandatory outcome viewpoints). However, while this option eliminates many of the problems noted above, it also is likely to present challenges for candidates. Perhaps the main challenge is the suspicion that the candidate does not want to disclose their fuller character or positions on issues, are hiding something, or just simply are not fit enough to be a bold and transparent leader, which is precisely what many constituents are yearning for in a candidate.

All that said, there will inevitably be polarizers and extremists that come through any political process who will appeal to a certain portion of the populace. But the aim of these protocols of civility is not to reach everyone, which is an impossible task for any proceeding. The aim is to reach the critical mass of voters that I believe is still out there, who not only wants civility in their candidates but a notable degree of empathy, caring, and dignity; for it is these qualities that are of utmost importance when "push comes to shove," such as the question of whether many of us will live or die. And many people, the research shows, share that sense of utmost importance, especially when they are not manipulated by fear-based media pundits, lobby-driven politicians, and corporate con artists. In fact, the research shows that a healthy cross-section of both liberals and conservatives share much more in common than they realize, and if they would just talk to each other and give each other the space to become more acquainted with each other, they would increase the likelihood of achieving some actionable common goals.[7]

The second process requirement takes effect after successful candidates are elected to office. This requirement entails an OPA-facilitated—supportive, structured—dialogue between representatives of opposing parties prior to any major legislative proceeding. The only exception to this requirement would be the need for emergency legislative action in the face of immediate peril, such as a direct military attack or adverse weather event. The question as to whether a legislative issue is "major" would be determined by either the minority or majority leaders of the respective parties engaged in the dialogue. The format of the dialogues would ideally be supportive, structured one-on-one encounters in private settings. In this instance, there would be less need for the entirety of the dialogues to be recorded so long as the outcomes—agreement and disagreement on the specific policy issues—are made publicly available. That said, it would be up to the dialogue partners to decide in advance if they wish to provide the partial or full recording of their encounters to the public. But both dialogue partners would have to agree on such disclosures; otherwise they would be prohibited from public consumption.

The protocol of civility would also be applied to the U.S. diplomatic corps. All diplomats serving the U.S. government's Diplomatic Affairs Division would be required to engage in EDD or related dialogue formats not only as a criterion for their eligibility for the corps but also, once employed, as a methodology in the practice of their diplomacy. As we know from other dialogue settings, awareness of knee-jerk reactions, biases, and ideological rhetoric is a critical first step in bracketing them and making conscious decisions to draw on a larger repertoire of engagement. Among the elements of this larger repertoire are the emphasis on genuine curiosity, openness, and respect toward the "other side." And, again, if this respect is not accorded to the other's ideology per se, at the least it should be accorded to the human being who is actively before one, willing to listen, and willing to be as vulnerable as possible, given the circumstances.

The OPA would also provide consultation, counseling, or any other nonsectarian advice at the behest of any member of the judiciary, legislative, or executive branches. The OPA is there to help officers of the government make the best, most psychologically informed decisions possible, both in the service of officers' individual lives as well as the lives of the nation they serve. Periodically, the OPA would distribute a newsletter summarizing key findings in the cultivation of vibrantly centered, emotionally restorative relationships for parents and families, schools and training agencies, work settings, spiritual and religious settings, medical settings, community environments, first responders and crisis situations, and legislative–diplomatic arenas. This also means that the OPA would need specialists across a very wide range of sectors to address the corresponding range of psychospiritual problems that have arisen.

Speaking of psychospiritual, it is imperative that the OPA provide field officers who address the expanding spiritual crisis in our society. These "existential" healers would treat the big picture issues, such as how to find meaning in the face of death or loss or how to keep faith in a society that degrades people on the basis of race or class. This challenge requires expertise in emotionally restorative relationships for multicultural as well as mainstream populations. The significance of this component of the OPA can't be underestimated. Many of the problems in our society stem from just these existential and spiritual deficits and they are essential to prioritize. Among the practices that such existential healers would provide are greater attention to religious and spiritual dimensions of peoples' issues in affordable, accessible psychotherapy. Among these issues: How do people cope with an increasingly technocratic and culturally fragmented world, and what do positive coping strategies look like? One of the coping strategies suggested by researchers of some minoritized and underserved populations, for example, is an openness to exploring the possibilities for a "warm and supportive relationship with a spiritual force" that provides hope, where such hope feels absent in peoples' daily lives.[8] This exploration can be particularly important in communities of color where the history of dehumanization will not readily abate.

Multicultural and Spiritual Support

The dimension of spirituality alerts us to the fact that there is a range of emotionally restorative relationships beyond the settings discussed so far that may be pertinent to the healing of diverse groups. Among these relationships are group formats that draw from the civil rights tradition such as the Community Healing Network's "Emotional Emancipation Circles." These circles emphasize deep respect for African traditions of psychological liberation, from the indigenous practice of "Sawubona—which means "I see you" and "I see your humanity"—extending to the teachings of Martin Luther King.[9] Still other groups utilize experiential tools such as mindfulness to facilitate multicultural healing.[10] The issue here is for the OPA to be prepared for a variety of bona fide approaches to deal with a range of communal needs.

To coordinate all these activities, the OPA would need to be managed by a culturally diverse steering committee and probably a Psychological Advisor-in-Chief or a Psychologist-General.[11] This psychospiritual leader would preside on a par with the present Surgeon General, who chiefly oversees medical and physician-centered care. That said, there would, of course, be need for communication and consultation across governmental and other allied agencies. For example, the OPA would need to be in regular contact with the Surgeon General, the Substance Abuse and Mental Health Services Administration (or SAMSHA), the National Institutes of Health (NIH) and Mental Health (NIMH), the Centers for Disease Control and Prevention (CDC), and the Health and Human Services (HHS) Department of the government, which oversees all such agencies.

The OPA would also need a very large assembly of personnel adequate to the range and variety of services that have been outlined above. Helping professionals in the private sector would also be recruited to the extent possible to make psychospiritual health as accessible and available as possible throughout the country. In many ways, we're talking about an agency on the scale of the Public Works Program of the Roosevelt administration in the 1930s, with an equivalent firmness of purpose. We're also talking about an agency that has the potential to improve many lives, and as with the Public Works program, to enhance the moral and even financial standing of the country. The more that people feel psychospiritually met, the greater the likelihood that they will be motivated to value themselves, others, and life as a whole; and the more that this evolves, the greater the likelihood that people will pursue employment that nourishes the communities they serve as well as themselves. Moreover, this is a self-reinforcing cycle. As noted earlier in the chapter on the vibrant center of work, the more employees are satisfied with both their lifestyles and jobs, the more they tend to consistently engage those lifestyles and jobs, and the greater their motivation to be productive, creative, and sociable.

Partnering with the Private Sector

The OPA is also in an optimal position to coordinate its services with private sector groups that are also fostering emotionally restorative relationships. For example, the Corps of Depth Healers created by the author of this book and assisted by doctoral student Tyler Gamlen is a resource for a range of helping professionals to enhance their abilities to apply depth principles of practice to social issues. The Corps includes a YouTube channel and a podcast called "Depth Dialogues" that features interviews with leading depth practitioners who apply their skills to social problems. A website—https://www.corpsofdepthhealers.com—features a certificate program in the art and practice of in-depth social healing. Below are the Vision and Mission statements of the

Corps of Depth Healers, which, as can be seen, are highly compatible with the proposed mandate of the OPA.

Vision of the Corps of Depth Healers Certificate Program

Numerous global threats, such as wars, cultural and political unrest, climate change, mass migration, and pandemics, seem to elude the effective responses of both governments and standardized healthcare. The emerging movement of the Corps of Depth Healers, on the other hand, suggests an innovative solution for our nation: fostering emotionally restorative relationships. Emotionally restorative relationships are those in which people feel seen and heard and that get at the roots of their problems. These relationships are essential in our view to address the emotionally impoverished relationships that underlie and inform many of our current problems.

There are many reasons for this impoverishment, from financial stress to dependence on technology to the quick fix/instant results we are growing to expect. But at their core lies the inability of our society to provide the substantive and enduring connections that lead to a more caring and supportive collective. Thus, the Corps of Depth Healers (https://www.corpsofdepthhealers.com) constitutes a coalition of like-minded healers and organizations committed to establishing emotionally restorative relationships as the norm in our democratic republic, a fundamental requirement for its sustainability.

Mission of the Corps of Depth Healers Certificate Program

In accordance with its vision, the Corps of Depth Healers represents a consortium of trained service providers whose aim is to provide affordable and accessible "emotionally restorative relationships" throughout the U.S. By emotionally restorative relationships, we mean relationships where people feel heard and seen, and that get at the roots of their problems. We also mean "healers" who are skilled in working with implicit as well as explicit psychosocial challenges. These service providers include but are not limited to psychologists, psychiatrists, social workers, physicians, nurses, counselors, mentors, life-coaches, educators, clergy, and other compassionate individuals who have undergone an organized course of study in healing communication.

These service providers are willing to dedicate a portion of their relational care to underserved communities or individuals at little or no cost. Included in these relational offerings are in-depth, longer term psychotherapy, intensive mentoring and school counseling, person-centered medical care, holistic organizational consulting, and humanistic conflict mediation that stress humane and civil dialogue between people holding contrasting cultural or political views.

The Corps hosts both a YouTube channel and a website. The YouTube channel showcases video examples of depth healers describing and applying their expertise to address a diverse array of social crises. These issues encompass cultural and political divisions, gun violence, religious conflicts, the COVID-19 pandemic, Zionism, racism, and authoritarianism.

The channel also addresses the crises in healthcare, organizational functioning, the ecosystem, and numerous other topics. The Corps website is a publicly accessible meeting ground where like-minded relational healers post summaries of their offerings, links to their websites and media, updates on current and future offerings, and ideas about the present and future needs of the Corps.

Summary of a Braver Angels Format

Another private sector organization that resonates with OPA aims is Braver Angels. Braver Angels not only provides conflict mediation workshops for everyday people in communities throughout the United States but also has a satellite program called "Braver Politics." Braver Politics directly addresses polarization among liberal and conservative legislators utilizing a format similar to the Braver Angels workshops in communities (see https://braverangels.org/politics/ for more details). Drawing from strict ground rules emphasizing openness, curiosity, and respect, speaking from one's own perspective rather than from party talking points, and bringing one's best self in attempting to learn about and understand the other, Braver Politics has brought adversarial legislators together for dialogues in several states. Although this program is relatively new, it has shown some promising results among the groups who have engaged it. Here's how one workshop proceeded in the New Hampshire House of Representatives on December 19, 2024:

The Workshop – Managing Difficult Conversations with Colleagues

The lead facilitators were Paul Catsos and Beth Malow, experienced Braver Angels moderators. They were assisted by Braver Angels' Coordinators for New

> Hampshire (NH), Brian MacDonald and Pat Calley as well as volunteer Lyn Leddy.
> [The] workshop goals were (1) To show people who disagree with you that they have been heard, (2) To find areas of commonality or agreement when those are present, (3) To share your views in a way that is likely to be heard by the other person. Ground rules were also reviewed and agreed upon: (1) We're here to talk about skills, not policies, so let's avoid policy debates; and (2) Let's help each other out as we work on the skills. It's not a competition.
>
> The workshop emphasized interactions among legislators. After reflection on specific questions or prompts, legislators were given an opportunity to discuss questions or practice skills in pairs with a partner. For all these exercises, they were encouraged to find partners whom they did not know, preferably not from their own political party. We then conducted group shares, so that participants could share their responses with the entire group.

At the start of the group the participants were asked why they attended, and here are several responses:

> "Until you can argue both sides, you are prejudiced. We are here to make decisions...need to look at all the dimensions...want to learn as much as I can."

> "Helpful to think of ourselves as a citizen legislature not by party, but all here to do work, find agreement when we can and if we can't, at least be civil."

> "I want to do everything I can to be civil, sometimes humorous, and try to work collaboratively as much as we can."

The key communication principles that were presented included:

1. Connect first, then share your view.
2. Aim for "accurate disagreement" instead of "distorted disagreement."
3. Focus on policy and not underlying motives; assume good intentions unless proven otherwise.
4. Strive to be consistent: If you practice principles 1 through 3 in person but not in your caucus, home district, and on social media, you will lose credibility.

The following communication skills were introduced and practiced during the workshop.

> **Listen** – focus both on the other's viewpoint and their underlying values and concerns.
> **Acknowledge** – a brief paraphrase of the person's view goes a long way for them to feel heard.
> **Agree** – find something to agree with, if possible, as this can build collegiality.
> **Perspective** – focus on "I" statements such as "This is how I see it"; mention values and concerns that the person likely shares and avoid negative labels and "us versus them" language...
> Legislators added the importance of tone of voice and body language when listening and responding to others.

At the close of the workshop, participants were asked: How do I hope to use these skills to work better with my colleagues here at the legislature? Here is a sampling of their responses:

> "In my world, people hold views similar to me. I know I need to work on committees with everybody and I think this is going to help me get along with other people and learn what other people's views are to appropriately discuss a bill and decide if we should pass it or not."

> "To build consensus among people...to work together to do what's for the best of the state."

Here is some of the key learning that legislators derived from the workshop:

> "Learning to listen and engage in a positive manner, look for common ground."

> "Remembering to listen attentively, respectfully and work to build consensus."

> "I utilized skills and took a risk to meet new people."

> "Listen, listen, listen! Listen first then speak. Reps tend to talk too much."

> "Personal connection [is] critically important to a respectful democratic process."

> "I enjoyed meeting colleagues from the other party. It is the first step to consensus building."

> "I'm sure what I learned will give me an advantage as a successful bipartisan legislator."

> "I believe we can be civil even when things are bad. We have to work together—makes it less stressful and difficult."[12]

While some of these responses may sound a bit simplistic, they are nevertheless real-life commentaries from a group of seasoned policy-makers who viewed the workshop as strikingly valuable.

Another private sector program that directly bolsters the OPA mandate is called "A Home Within." A Home Within is a nationally sponsored nonprofit that provides free in depth psychotherapy to foster children and adults who have been foster children. The program comprises a range of multicultural practitioners who devote a portion of their time to providing longer-term, relational, and psychodynamic therapy to this underserved population. To get a fuller sense of A Home Within's objectives, here is their mission statement (https://www.ahomewithin.org/about-us/mission-history/) excerpted from their website:

A Home Within: Free Therapy for Foster Youth

A Home Within provides transformative mental health care to foster youth while building the field of the future.

A Home Within is a community-driven solution to the youth mental health crisis.

We don't depend on government grants or insurance company contracts. We don't wait for the system to provide youth what they deserve. We transcend policy, bureaucracy, politics, and economic cycles.

At A Home Within, we understand the profound impact a single, lasting relationship has in the life of someone impacted by foster care.

There is no time limit. No age limit. No red tape. Youth choose their therapist and continue "for as long as it takes."

There are a number of other private sector programs that foster emotionally supportive relationships at no or comparatively low cost. Among these are Starts with Us, Nonviolent Communications, Arnie and Amy Mindell's Worldwork, Waging Dialogues, the Israeli–Palestinian Living Room Dialogue Group and the Existential Movement. Each of these groups appears to be highly dedicated to cultivating a vibrantly centered consciousness that could be significantly bolstered by OPA resources and networks.

Vibrantly-Centered Governance: A Summary of Proposed Outcomes

Finally, here is a point-by-point summary of proposed outcomes for a vibrantly-centered, psychospiritually informed, government:

- The expansion and enhancement of mental and spiritual support services throughout the United States.
- The improvement and affordability of such care for underserved populations
- The improvement and affordability of such care for diverse populations
- The provision of a higher quality of care that is linked to the research on personality and therapeutic effectiveness
- The enhancement of the general psychological well-being of the U.S. population (and by implication global well-being, sustainability)
- The improvement of physical well-being as a result of such psychological enhancement
- The improvement of social consciousness and conscientiousness as a result of the enhancement of psychological well-being; and the reduction thereby of weapons of mass destruction both domestically and in the conduct of military operations overseas.

- The improvement of productivity and social-organizational functioning (including at the top levels of government) as a result of such psychological enhancement
- The improvement of the ability to adapt to adverse circumstances as a result of such psychological enhancement
- The enhancement of the influence of the helping professions in the everyday lives of the U.S. populace
- The assurance that nonmedical psychological resources and applications will continue to flourish and evolve
- The expansion of "whole person" or integrative healthcare

Chapter 6

Are We Ready for a Political Party Called the "Vibrant Center"?

Are we ready for a political party that prioritizes a vibrant center of consciousness for our society; a party that stresses presence, openness, and discernment toward self and others; a pivot point of individual and collective choice, deliberation, and discovery in all major sectors of our lives? If we are ready for such a party, and I think we must be in these devitalized times when the U.S. public's choice between Democrats and Republicans impoverishes our souls as well as economic viability, then there is no time to waste. We need a Vibrant Center Party! (See the poll showing that a growing number of young Americans are rejecting the two main parties.)[1]

What might a Vibrant Center Party stand for beyond presence, openness, and discernment?

First, it would stand for leaders who promote dialogue and not dogma, who act responsibly, not essentially from fear or insecurity but from mindful and heartful deliberation and concern for human flourishing. It follows then that, first and foremost, we simply have to bring sanity to the gun and weaponry availability in our country. The tools of autocratic leaders and their followers—weapons of mass destruction—simply have to be more vigorously controlled, just as in virtually every other contemporary democracy. Those "tools" must also be kept out of the hands of people with established records of gun violence and physical assault. It's a basic issue: We can't have anything resembling a democratic republic—a republic prizing freedoms of speech, opinions, media, faith, inquiry, study, creativity, and mobility—if we are perpetually harassed by people carrying guns and an astounding variety of automatic weapons. We can't have a proper right of assembly in such circumstances, access to independent and balanced news, reliable sources of information, vigorous debate and dialogue, rigorous inquiry and many other rights that we have taken for granted over our 250-year experiment. There's just no way that people will feel safe to express themselves and question leaders if they relentlessly fear for their safety either by the leaders themselves or the fanatics who purport to carry out their interests. Such an ethos shuts down the whole operation of investigation and discovery—two of the pillars of democracy and enhancement of lives.

Think about it: What protesters will express their full opinions to policy-makers in the face of constant threats to their existence? What students will pursue their deepest inquiries knowing that other students have the power to destroy them with one pull of a trigger? What news outlets, legislators, spiritual and religious leaders, philosophers, and scientists will express their methodically developed knowledge in the face of a flurry of implied threats to remove them or their loved ones from earthly existence? Few, I would say, and the costs of such a fallout are mounting in this weapon-obsessed, regulation-scarce country.

Correspondingly, a Vibrant Center Party would endorse a social capitalist or social democratic form of government, akin to such governments in parts of northern Europe such as Norway and Denmark. This is a government that balances the need for material acquisition and a modicum of wealth with equal needs for a social safety net—low-cost medical care, education, and housing. The provision of a standard of moral decency, in other words, is integral to a safer, more stable and fulfilled populace. By contrast, a hyper-individualist, hyper-consumerist approach, which pervades our world today, continually puts our country and world on the brink. Maslow called the basis for this hyper-acquisitive orientation "deficiency" motivation as distinct from "being"-motivation (or at least momentum toward being-motivation), which places more emphasis on quality of living rather than quantity or financial status.[2] Moreover, it's precisely being-motivation that fuels the vibrant center of presence, openness, and discernment—a discovery or awe-based orientation more than a scrambling or fear-based orientation. Such a social democratic position also fuels the opportunity for appreciation of the many sides of our individual and collective lives, and the responsibility we bear for attunement to those many sides—attunement to proportionality in the distribution of resources, job training, and diverse forms of cultural and political expression; attunement to the consequences of tradition, the health of the planet, the beauty and sustainability of the planet, the beauty and sustainability of human inquiry, exploration, and awe.

Indeed, such a framework would impose greater sacrifices on those blessed with higher incomes and material possessions and would likely entail a progressive tax rate, as esteemed economists from Robert Reich to Joseph Stiglitz have called for.[3] It would also encourage fuller employment and reduced economic hardship for many, as economist Janet Yellen has called for.[4] And it would encourage meaningful and creative employment, as Thierry Pauchant, Wendy Smith, and Marianne Lewis have advocated.[5]

But I propose that a Vibrant Center platform would also be sympathetic to those economists and policy-makers who support robust investment in more traditional areas of the U.S. economy, such as innovation in manufacturing, transportation, housing, urban design, drug development, and competitiveness in science and technology. The Vibrant Center platform would also recognize the value of other American traditions, such as the close ties of family, cultural tradition and ritual, and religion—but ever with an eye to gleaning the best from these traditions. And by "best" I mean the aspects of traditions that are genuinely centered on choice and discernment and that embrace paradoxes of living.[6] This means, as I've suggested earlier, that authoritative parenting would be encouraged over either hyper-permissive or authoritarian parenting. In this context, kids would be encouraged to express their physical selves in contact with sports and nature as much as their mental and spiritual selves in contact with schools and places of worship. It would also mean the support of cultural traditions and rituals that promote nonviolent and nondogmatic inquiry, dialogue, and travel as well as movement, dance, music, and many other rich and varied forms of expression. It would further mean the encouragement of religious and spiritual groups that prize the sustainment of life and mystery of existence; that prioritize basic principles of humility, wonder, and charity toward self and others; and that vigorously uphold the dignity of the nonhuman plant and animal world as well as that of the human. It would support individual and collective choice in response to extremely ambiguous circumstances, such as the decision of whether or when it may be necessary to abort an unborn child (as the American Medical Association and other allied organizations have advocated). And it would promote nonsectarian psychological, spiritual, and medical counseling to help with such decisions as well as equivalent facilities to care for parents and children in the aftermath of such decision-making.

A Vibrant Center Party would recognize "nuggets of truth"—and even richness in both traditional and progressive tendencies. The slippery slope of conflation—or the equation of a few ideas or people with an entire ideology or group—would be conspicuously avoided. The emphasis wouldn't be that "they have some contemptible ideas, and therefore their worldview is contemptible," or "they committed some heroic acts, therefore their party is heroic." Rather, a Vibrant Center Party would emphasize "how our party can understand and learn from elements of their party and ideology so that we have a more inclusive and ennobling party ourselves."

In the circumstance of war or defense of the country, a Vibrant Center platform would advocate for a coalition of executive, legislative, military, medical, and psychospiritual decision-makers, short of an emergency, of course, which would then demand quick action with the hope that the executive who takes that action is informed by the presence, openness, and discernment with which they have spent a lifetime grappling. That said, the principle of accelerated action in the face of increasing urgency still holds. The more that adversaries threaten the life or lives of others, the less that presence, openness, and discernment are relevant and the more that transactional assertiveness becomes pertinent. This, sadly, may be the case in the "mean streets" of towns and cities (assuming the circumstances are real and not hyped up for political purposes) but also in the context of major wars. Take the present clash between Israel and Palestine as an example. As of this writing, it appears that the "muscular" policies of U.S. President Donald Trump toward both Palestinian and Israeli leadership may actually lead to a lasting cease-fire, along with the potential for a lasting and viable peace, although the latter prospect is still a very long way off.

It also appears that Trump's forceful approach was viable in this circumstance. Think what one will about Trump—and I sympathize with those who view him as autocratic, it is also tragically plausible that some of those very tendencies are necessary to quell even greater expressions of such destructiveness. (Think also of U.S. General Patton's "slash and burn" policy of decimating Nazis toward the end of World War II or of U.S. President Bill Clinton's bombardment campaign to end the mass destruction of the Serbian war, and so on). Such scenarios bring up the egregious problem of cycles of polarization. The more the cycles escalate, the less that centeredness and vibrancy matter, and the more that hardness and force become the necessary options. That is precisely why we need to limit such derangements in the first place by supporting leaders who help us work through rather than amplify escalating differences. Of course, it is also possible for a more or less vibrantly centered leader to exercise autocratic authority at points—as I believe Roosevelt and Eisenhower did during World War II. Desperate times call for desperate measures, but—in stark contrast to the tendencies of many parties throughout history, including today—it is certainly not a habitual style that a Vibrant Center party would either encourage or enable. By contrast, a Vibrant Center party would advocate that while strong-arm leadership may be necessary under certain conditions, it needs to be rapidly and methodically contained, for as history has taught us repeatedly "might makes right" is a catastrophic long-term plan.[7]

Unfortunately, this latter scenario may be playing out with Trump's decision to start a war with Iran. As many of us know, at least in terms of what we've experienced over the past century, countries do not have an admirable record when it comes to starting wars—preemptive or otherwise. Beating another nation into submission, even if on the face of it to prevent future (and too often fantasized) perils, has led to many unforeseen backlashes. Think of the U.S. incursion into Korea and North Korea's subsequent acquisition of a nuke; the debacle in Viet Nam, where hundreds of thousands were killed only to result in failure; the backlashes from the CIA-backed installation of the Shah of Iran, which led to a theocratic revolt; the ill-conceived invasion of Iraq, eventuating in ISIS; and on and on. And this list does not even include the disastrous incursions by Nazi Germany into Europe, Japan into China, and most recently Russia into Ukraine. In each of these scenarios, reactivity and grandiosity trumped rigorous and longer term diplomacy, which in our modern era, with so much access to destructive weaponry, would seem the wisest path to follow—again, short of an emergency (which must be a very carefully considered term!).

A Vibrant Center party must also be ready, as best as possible, to deal with the onslaught of technology and the AI revolution. The chief issue here becomes one of *how* the technology is approached—how present, open, and discerning one can be toward its use. Thus, some of the concerns the Vibrant Center party might rally around would be: Can the technology free us from mundane tasks such as cleaning our clothes, washing our dishes, transporting us, ensuring that we take the right medicines so that we can focus on tasks that matter even more to us? Among these tasks might be the development of a craft or work of art, the promotion of a gratifying person-to-person relationship, and/or the enhancement of our physical environment, the improvement of our healthcare, the enrichment of our education, and the creation of communities that are more livable, sustainable, and meaningful.[8] Another concern might be how we can use technology to better understand and "build bridges" with one another, whether among those who are mentally and physically limited or between populations of diverse cultural, geographic, and linguistic backgrounds.

Can we use machines to refine our ability to better understand and preserve what is unique to our humanity? Can machines be used as reference points for what is both debilitating and enlivening about the lives we lead and the kind of societies we seek to design? Can we use technology to supplement, not replace, human skills and resources? Can we collaborate with machines, for example, to enhance our capacity to be deeply moved, either through discoveries in art, science, and religion–spirituality or through our everyday capacity to experience nature, our own bodies, and our own capacities for wonder and discovery? These are but a few of the perspectives that a vibrantly centered, present, open, and discerning political party are likely to prioritize in the face of onrushing mechanization.

In sum, the stances I have outlined for a vibrantly centered political party are suggestive. There is no utopian roadmap for any of them. They are all provisional, and they are all risks. But they are risks derived from deep and many-sided deliberations, deliberations that are likely to be more substantive and encompassing than the current ethos of quick fix/instant result reactivity that possesses neither the intellect nor heart of the former. The deliberations, moreover, would be informed and supported by like-minded bodies of leadership, such as the previously mentioned Office of Psychological Advisors and the growing sectors of community that benefit from a vibrant center of consciousness.

What then are the platforms of a Vibrant Center Party? Here is a summary of my recommendations (which draw in part on the recommendations of writers, journalists, social scientists, and everyday people):

Philosophy

- First and foremost: Embrace a vibrant center of consciousness—presence to self and others, openness to people and ideas, and discernment about the values and directions one adopts.
- Related to the above: Appreciate the paradoxes of life—our capacities to constrict and expand and our abilities to respond to and integrate those capacities as distinct from reacting against and segregating those capacities. This dynamic ability is fostered by presence (the holding and illuminating of that which is palpably significant within oneself and toward others), life-enhancing anxiety (the capacity to live more on the edge of wonder and discovery than terror and overwhelm), and a sense of awe (the humility and wonder, sense of adventure) toward life.
- Be aware that freedom encompasses responsibility. The more free one becomes the more one becomes aware of the interconnections one has with caretakers, culture, institutions, and traditions and the more one gains the capacity to experience life in-depth. And the more one becomes aware of these contexts, the greater one's tendency to want to improve these connections for the benefit of all.

Policies

- Support for a U.S. Office of Psychological Advisors to inform the psychospiritual well-being of the government and populace.
- Support for political leaders who emphasize the value of dialogue and emotionally restorative relationships across all major sectors of our society.
- Support for bona fide private sector organizations that promote affordable and accessible emotionally restorative relationships.
- Support for gun controls that significantly reinstill peoples' trust in nonviolent assembly, dialogue and debate, political and cultural coexistence, and civil society.
- Support for a Nordic-style social democracy that mixes a free market economy with significant social safety nets such as quality low-cost housing, healthcare, education, and job training—and that fosters such a policy through progressive taxation.
- Support for meaning-based, worker-controlled businesses as well as businesses that include psychological and physiological well-being programs, supportive counseling and coaching, and attunement to community needs.
- Support for living wages and greater proportionality between workers and management.
- Support for closing pay gaps based on race, gender, and other characteristics unrelated to the job setting. Support for merit-based employment coupled with ample opportunities for job training and specialization.
- Support for environmental well-being, and concrete action to address climate change.
- Support for stricter limits on donations to political campaigns.
- Support for viewpoint diversity in schools and universities.

- Support in the form of job training or re-specialization for workers whose jobs are being replaced by high tech and changing trends in the marketplace.
- Support for early education such as Head Start for underserved communities
- Support for bona fide qualitative and quantitative science to help guide mental and physical health programs
- Support for the restoration of philosophy, critical thinking, the arts and humanities, and physical education in schools
- Support for community-friendly urban environments that stress affordable housing, humane and aesthetically pleasing architecture, access to mass transit, walkable streets, low-emission vehicles, and health-conscious community centers
- Support for strong national borders but also thoughtful, welcoming paths to citizenship for hardworking or oppressed people from abroad
- Support for carefully deliberated conservative and liberal values and the search for common ground

Groups Likely to Join

I believe with *New York Times* and *Atlantic* columnist David Brooks that "America Needs a Mass movement—Now"![9] While a Vibrant Center Party is not likely to attract either left or right extremists, I do think there are many aspects of the party platform that will appeal to a vast range of people in between. These people include liberals, conservatives and swing and independent voters who are increasingly exasperated by the extremists and eager for a new paradigm. I also think that swing voters and some of the more independent-minded coalitions that have arisen in recent years, such as the conflict mediation group Braver Angels, as well as the No Labels and Indivisible movements, would view many elements of a Vibrant Center party as compatible with or even accentuating their core values. Among these values are a stress on independence, openness, and discernment concerning the selection of given political candidates; the prizing of an awe-based or spiritual component to the party; the support for affordable healthcare as well as a government office—the OPA—devoted strictly to enhancing the mental health of our citizens and government employees themselves; the prioritizing of our mental and spiritual well-being on a par with our military and materialist well-being; the rebalancing of an economic system that has too long catered to the rich and corporatocracy and that puts vital funds back in the hands of everyday people in order for them to attain decent wages, healthcare, education, and housing; and a party that prizes dialogue and understanding of the diverse communities of the United States as distinct from one that manipulates and imposes ideological propaganda on them. I also believe that such constituencies would appreciate the paradoxical nature of the Vibrant Center platforms: its stress on *both* experimentation and safety; human limits *as well as* creativity; safety nets (healthcare, education, housing), *and* encouragement to train, work, and innovate; religion/spirituality *and* openness to science and the arts; allowance of gun ownership *and* strict controls on how they are used; freedom of speech *and* careful deliberation about whom it impacts; a life of inquiry, wonder *and* practicality, innovation, and so on. Simply put, there are many attractive features in this dynamically centered position for a striking range of people along the political spectrum. One can only hope that people will begin reaching for it, making it an unprecedented life-path.

Chapter 7

Toward an Awe-Based, Vibrantly Centered World

I've hinted at it before, but now it's time to make it plain. The chief purpose of vibrantly centered governance and, indeed, this book is to promote "awe-based consciousness." By awe-based consciousness, I mean awareness that is centered in the humility and wonder, thrill and anxiety of living. This is an awareness that brings dynamism and depth to the "life, liberty, and pursuit of happiness" clause in our Declaration of Independence—the sense of adventure, not only adaptation in our day-to-day realities.

Awe-based consciousness opens us up to the poignancy of life as well as pleasure, our capacity to be deeply moved as well as content, and our capacity for presence and openness as well as discernment. In short, awe-based consciousness is our contemporary declaration of independence—or better yet "interdependence;" it prizes fullness of living as well as ease, risk and relationship as well as solitude.

Resilience: Key to Awe-Based, Vibrantly Centered Communities

If we want to gain insight into an awe-based, vibrantly centered society, we need to look at the individuals and groups that exhibit such qualities. These people range from the "ordinary" laborer to the exotic artist, from technicians to philosophers. But the through-line among all these individuals is that they possess varying degrees of what many today term "resilience." The resilient do not just survive but also thrive in the face of turbulence and loss. We have already mentioned extraordinary individuals such as Viktor Frankl, Nelson Mandela, Maya Angelou, and Stephen Hawking as exemplars, but what about more "everyday" people who hold everyday jobs and lead ordinary lives? Arguably, these are the people most representative of larger populations, and who in the long run may be the best models for awe-based, society-wide change. To be sure, many of these people have suffered greater trials than the average person, but, as will become clear, those trials are not at all alien to most of us; they are merely more intense. For who among us has not suffered profound losses, difficult home lives, and vexing financial circumstance? Who has not toiled with primal fears of groundlessness and helplessness, the unknown and the foreign? The difference between the respective groups, therefore, is more one of degree rather than of kind, and, as we shall see, their respective remedies for their problems share much in common (see also Appendix B).

Therefore, if we can gain insight into how the unusually resilient live, we will by implication gain insight into how a vibrantly centered, awe-based society can live, for such a society must also by definition maximize resilience.

Stories of Resilient Research Participants

To explore how resilient people live, let's start with the in-depth investigations of Harvard-trained psychologist and researcher Gina O' Connell Higgins. In a now classic study, she defined resilient people as those who have suffered "significant challenges" at critical points of their lives but were able to "snap back." To pursue her inquiry more intimately, O'Connell Higgins interviewed 40 research participants from the Greater Boston area. These participants had suffered many trials in childhood and adolescence including, in varying degrees, "serious illness themselves or [in] their families, low income, chronic family discord...parental substance abuse, persistent and harsh parental discipline, [and] prolonged parental absence." In addition, "over half her participants "had a history of repeated physical and/or sexual abuse."[1]

In order to characterize her participants as resilient, O'Connell Higgins set stringent criteria:

- They establish and maintain relationships marked by a high degree of reciprocity and concern for the other as well as the self
- They develop and actively participate in relationships that can withstand (or even thrive on) conflict, disappointment, frequent anger, and frustration when the needs of either person in the relationship are not met. These conflicts are actively and successfully negotiated throughout each relationship.
- They relate to others in a way that, in general, does not sacrifice the accuracy and empathy with which they perceive other people; that is, they make consistent and generally successful attempts to recognize the needs and characteristics of others and to differentiate those needs from their own.

Moreover, and not least, these participants knew how to "love well." They all reported "satisfying intimate love relationships for an average of twelve and a half years" in a "1984 group (n=23) and eighteen years" in a later "1992 group (n=17)."[2]

In order to obtain her participants, O'Connell Higgins contacted over 30 clinicians (licensed psychologists and licensed independent social workers) and with their help located the 40 participants selected for the study. Demographics-wise there was a comparatively even divide among men and women, whose average age was 40. Despite efforts to reach more diverse populations, her sample was predominantly White, which constituted a notable limitation of her research. On the other hand, the participants were diverse with regard to their religious, cultural, and economic backgrounds—though by the time of the study most were middle to upper class and made more money than their parents.

Aside from the fact that 80% of O'Connell Higgins' participants were or had been in psychotherapy for two years or longer, perhaps the most striking feature of this study from the standpoint of a vibrant-centered, awe-based society, were the "surrogates" that 36 of the 40 participants encountered at critical stages of their lives. These surrogates or "helpful witnesses," as Alice Miller conceived them,[3] came from many walks of life. They included friends, peers, teachers, grandparents, and others who had often been through significant difficulties themselves but who worked hard toward becoming whole. The sense of *wholeness*, in fact, was a key dimension in the evolution of participants' resilience.

How, specifically, were the surrogates helpful? O'Connell-Higgins concluded that they provided a "good enough holding environment" for the participants fortunate enough to encounter them. By holding environment, O'Connell Higgins echoed D.W. Winnicott's conception of a relational context in which the child or sufferer feels supported and understood or, to put it more concretely, heard and seen in a way that inspired their fuller capacities not only to cope with life but to pursue what deeply matters about life—their "highest level of functioning." These surrogates provided a "love," in other words, that may have spanned only "a few years, months, or even weeks" but that in many cases proved life transforming.[4] On this point, Rebecca Graber and her colleagues found that even one supportive relationship (such as a close friendship) from ages 11–19 could facilitate sustained resilience later in life.[5] This shows how even isolated instances of love can have remarkable impacts on relatively large ranges of individuals.

Put concretely, then, surrogates in both O'Connell Higgins' and Graber and colleague's studies conveyed to participants that "they were deeply special and important simply by being who they were."[6] Akin to Carl Rogers' "facilitative conditions" for effective psychotherapy, and in sharp contrast to many of the manipulative relationships participants had labored with for much of their early life, surrogates provided a nonpossessive warmth, genuineness, and empathy that gave participants a fundamental sense that life—and their lives in particular—really mattered and that change was possible. The participants made comments about their surrogates such as the following: "He [the surrogate] loved me for who I was; I didn't need to do anything to prove myself"; "She believed I was wonderful just because I existed"; "She was strict, but she made me feel that life was worth living"; "He had a home where a kid could be a kid"; and "There was never a time in all the years I knew her that she ever let me down....There was something I could always count on."[7]

Surrogates also "encouraged the resilient to let their talents unfold, whatever their strengths might be." In this sense, they also taught the resilient how to survive and potentially even thrive despite adverse circumstances. They conveyed, sometimes with their own flaws, that love could be both "disappointing and life-affirming simultaneously," and that "such complexity places a great premium on the resilient person's capacity to integrate irony since little that shines in their lives is undappled."[8]

Thus, in addition to their warmth, genuineness, and attunement, the surrogates in O'Connell Higgins' study also acknowledged life's contrasts and contradictions—the "good, the bad, and the ugly"—even in the best of us. And this big-picture view of life enabled the resilient to step back and appreciate life's absurdity at times, along with the humor, play, and sense of irony that keeps us afloat in spite of it. Indeed, participants described their surrogates as "figures with the stately grace of a steel suspension bridge," and as the "only 'whole' adults [they] encountered as young children,"[9] and, in many cases I would surmise, as adolescents and young adults as well.

O'Connell Higgins also found that based in large part on the healers and surrogates in their lives, the resilient participants were able to develop a trust or faith, not generally in some formal doctrine, but in humanity and existence. She quotes the prominent theologian Reinhold Niebuhr's criterion for "faith-full" human beings as those who give "themselves for that which is greater than themselves." She then goes on to describe the many ways this faith manifested in her resilient participants.

> Hence we need not look necessarily for a formal religious affiliation in the resilient, but we should find fierce fidelity in an anchored and elaborate vision of a more humane life. Germanely, most of my subjects found and still sustain their faith *outside* formal religious communities, although they are no less devout for their secularity.[10]

These observations resonate with the vibrantly centered, awe-based testimony we discussed earlier in connection with emerging forms of religion and spirituality. The growing population of people who feel unaligned with traditional forms of religion and spirituality could well relate to this resilient population's perspective. There is a great freedom in what I have called "faith in the inscrutable" or "enchanted agnosticism"[11] because they enable profound inquiries into the processes of creation that unshackle the mind and heart from orthodoxies that no longer inspire whole and vibrantly centered lives. With increasing frequency, it seems, many people are searching for forms of religion and spirituality that encourage inquiry, creative and timely ritual, and deep meditations on life. These forms increasingly address what deeply matters about one's own personal life as well as the life of one's family, culture, and world: How does one experience faith or trust in the radically unknown? And who or what should lead us on these quests?" The increasing emphasis on intercultural and interfaith exchanges yield insights into these foundational questions as they point us ever closer to a spirituality of humanity with all the tensions, joys, and discoveries that attend. For elaboration on these points, see Stephen Batchelor's *Buddhism Without Beliefs*, Paul Tillich's *Dynamics of Faith,* Rollo May's *Cry for Myth*, William James's *Variety of Religious Experience*, and my *Awakening to Awe.*[12]

O'Connell Higgins' participants also became more politically involved. Many of them engaged in political causes that countered the abuse and suffering they had experienced as children. Others were motivated to restore a general civility to society. Here's how one participant put it: "At least five days a week I spend all my time helping other people who had childhoods like my own...That's my whole life, not only my work....I go home at night and I can look at myself in the mirror and say, 'You did a lot of good for other people today.' It's become a crusade of joy."[13]

O'Connell-Higgins concludes: "Thus the most dramatic evidence to support my speculations about my subjects' depth of vision as well as the role of altruism in healing is the data that suggest that they actually *live* by their humanitarian convictions."[14]

In a major review of resilience studies, Masten confirmed many of O'Connell-Higgins' findings. Reflecting on the condition generally, she writes that resilience is associated with the following:

> effective parenting and caregiving; close relationships with other capable adults; close friends and romantic partners; intelligence and problem-solving skills; self-control, emotion regulation, planfulness; motivation to succeed; self-efficacy (or the sense of control and agency); faith, hope, belief that life has meaning; effective schools; effective neighborhoods, [and] "collective efficacy."[15]

Bonanno also noted that resilience is linked to nurturing relationships and the capacity for agency, flexibility, and control.[16] He also views resilience as more prevalent in our society than is often believed. In this sense, he views resilience and, by implication, the vibrant center and awe-based consciousness on a spectrum of intensity—cutting across cultures, classes, ethnicities, educational and work settings, and local environments.[17] Still, there is a difference between experiencing moments of resilience—such as coping effectively with a minor injury, or achieving an unexpectedly high grade, or even adjusting at one's job or marriage following a significant trauma—and cultivating a lifetime of resilience or deepening one's capacity for presence, openness, and discernment over years or even decades. This is the challenge I'm raising in this book: how such vibrant centeredness can become a life-philosophy that raises the quality of living for sustained periods of time over a diverse and sizeable population.

Stories of Resilient Luminaries

Although less representative of larger populations, the backgrounds of resilient luminaries are still a source of vital insight into awe-based, vibrant-centered consciousness. These luminaries may, in fact, represent the very best of such consciousness, and add to as well as reinforce the data we have on the backgrounds of the more typical subjects we call resilient. These luminaries also have more diverse and prominent profiles than the subjects we have described above, and so add to the depth and variety of resilient life-paths. Our focus here, therefore, will not so much be on the personality characteristics of these folks but on *how* they acquired these characteristics. This focus is critical if we are to learn more about how whole cultures and, indeed, how societies may optimize their levels of well-being.

We've already glimpsed the characteristics of luminaries like Viktor Frankl, Nelson Mandela, Maya Angelou, and Stephen Hawking as well as people Maslow conceived as deficient- versus being-motivated. Now, let's now look more closely at the background of these and other outstanding personalities. How did they become the people they grew up to be, and what do their life-paths inform us about the formation of a more vibrant-centered, awe-based world? It also should be noted that the succeeding testimonies are very much in keeping with Maslow's project to learn about what he described as "self-actualizing" personalities, with two major exceptions. First, the people I am about to describe not only have led self-actualizing lives, but they detailed such lives in both their philosophies and artistry. Second, they have also contributed explicitly to the social development of our world, and their works have lasting social significance.

Setting the Bar for Meaning in a World of Despair: Viktor Frankl (1905–1997)

Let's consider the development of Viktor Frankl, for example. What were the formative moments of his resilience as both Holocaust survivor and healer? Frankl was born into an upper middle class Austrian family. However, at the onset of World War I, conditions became so bad that he and his sister were forced to beg for food. Frankl's father, Gabriel Frankl, held a series of positions with the Austrian government, working primarily with the department of child protection and youth welfare. He was known as something of a perfectionist and instilled in his son the importance of being intensely rational and having a firm sense of social justice. Frankl described his mother, Elsa, as a kindhearted and deeply pious woman, but during his childhood she often described him as a pest and even changed the words of Frankl's favorite childhood lullaby to include calling him a pest. This may have been due to the fact that Frankl often asked questions, so much so that a family friend nicknamed him "The Thinker." From his mother, Frankl inherited a deep emotionality. One aspect of this emotionality involved a deep attachment to his childhood home, and he often felt homesick as his responsibilities kept him away. Moreover, those responsibilities began at an early age.[18]

Drawing upon his early abilities to cope with financial hardships, his growing confidence as a hard worker and scholar, and his ability to engage people with his observations about life, Frankl began to formulate his philosophy of meaning as a path to well-being. He gave talks on meaning in life as early as high school, and he wrote a paper in his late teens that came to the attention of psychoanalytic pioneer Sigmund Freud. In turn, Freud thought so highly of the paper that he promoted it for publication in the *International Journal of Psychoanalysis*. Although they met only once, Freud and Frankl corresponded for many years following the publication of Frankl's article.

Eventually, however, Frankl became disenchanted with key aspects of Freud's theories—namely, the pleasure principle, and began to gravitate toward another pioneer in Freud's circle, Alfred Adler. Frankl not only studied Adler's theories, he also got to know him personally and became a dedicated student in his seminars. Frankl was especially attracted to Adler's concept of "social interest" and its implications for social justice. However this enchantment also soon faded as Frankl found Adler's perspective limiting in key areas, and Adler in turn became distant from Frankl, eventually expelling him from his program.

After these critical experiences, Frankl struck out on his own and began to become a leader in socialist causes and existential approaches to therapy—particularly what he called "meaning"-oriented therapy, which in his view went beyond both Freudian and Adlerian approaches.[19]

What we can see from these reflections on Frankl's life is that like other resilient subjects, Frankl learned to cope with early adversity, and he applied this learning both in school as a stand-out scholar and as a champion of social justice. It is also clear that despite his parents' shortcomings, they supported him to work hard, to become educated, and to develop empathy for others who suffered. Surrogates also appeared to be pivotal to Frankl's life and career path. In Frankl's case these were remarkable figures such as the psychoanalysts Sigmund Freud and Alfred Adler. Although Frankl eventually parted ways with these luminaries, especially in the case of Adler, they undoubtedly proved critical to Frankl's confidence, discipline, and willingness to take personal and professional risks. In time, Frankl brought these qualities to his later battles with anti-semitism and, eventually, to the Nazi death camps, where, in contrast to everyone in his immediate family, he survived.[20]

Interpersonal Relations and Impact on Future Generations

Frankl was intensely committed to a social democratic vision of life. Although he accepted aspects of the capitalist system, he reportedly worked tirelessly to reform it through organizations such as "free youth counseling centers" in Vienna that "effectively" reduced rates of teen suicide. He also tried his best to provide humane and affordable medical services to his patients. In spite of many such contributions to society, however, Frankl also experienced some tensions with colleagues over concerns about "authoritarian" elements in his approach to patients as well as controversial aspects of his practice, which allegedly included psychosurgery.[21]

Still, there is no doubt of Frankl's lasting contributions to psychology and psychiatry, as noted by the remarkable durability of his theories, coupled with his extraordinary accounts of resilience in the Nazi death camps. His classic volume *Man's Search for Meaning* has been on bestseller lists for more than six decades and has been of profound value for many suffering souls.

From Survivor to Global Icon: Nelson Mandela (1918–2013)

Nelson Mandela grew up in a comparatively privileged South African family. His father was a Thembu chief and the principal counsellor to the acting king. After his father died, Mandela was sent to live in a royal palace. There, he grew up with the Regent's children and shared many of the privileges they enjoyed. Mandela's mother ensured that Mandela received a Methodist education. But Mandela also grew up with frequent exposure to the activities of the royal court, which formed an early understanding of the importance of hearing many sides of a given case, as well as the procedure of argumentation, which appeared to help equip him for the use of those skills in later life.

From his father, Mandela also learned about both the value and difficulty of hard work. His father was apparently quite stern in his treatment of his young charge and placed him in positions of notable responsibility as early as age five. One of these responsibilities was the management of livestock, which was painstaking for the young child, but also spiritually uplifting, as this particular task was viewed by Mandela's culture as comprising sacred and mystical elements, and genuine sources of joy. Still there is little doubt that the challenges of such labors along with the endurance he displayed before the rigors of strict parenting foreshadowed kindred qualities he drew upon later in life, and in particular during his 27 years in prison.

Despite his demanding side, Mandela's father also seemed to possess a very staunch feeling for social justice, and for the dignity of his indigenous fellow South Africans. For example, unlike some of his peers, Mandela's father stood up for the humanity of outgroups in his community. "When I was not much more than a newborn child," Mandela recalled, "my father was involved in a dispute that deprived him of his chieftainship at Mvezo and revealed a strain in his character I believe he passed on to his son [Mandela himself]. I maintain that nurture, rather than nature, is the primary molder of personality, but my father possessed a proud rebelliousness, a stubborn sense of fairness, that I recognize in myself."[22]

The dispute to which Mandela refers apparently centered on the treatment of outcasts (the amaMfengu brothers) within the community in which Mandela grew up. Yet, as Mandela elaborates: "My father didn't subscribe to local prejudice toward amaMfengu and he befriended two amaMfungu brothers, George and Ben Mbekela."

This robust sense of fairness seemed to radiate through the father's general philosophy toward society. According to Sithole, Mandela's father clearly did not hate other members of a racial background or ethnicity, even when it was popular to do so. This trait was passed on to Mandela as he fought to end racial oppression at a time when it was popular with those in power. Mandela, being of a royal background and educated, could have lived passively and not have chosen to fight in the struggle that became his life. However, thanks to role models like his father, who set the precedent as to how to treat others who are different, Mandela was able to stand up for what he believed in and make a positive impact on South Africa.

Mandela's tribal name was "Rolihlahala," which colloquially meant "trouble-maker." As Sithole observed:

> From his moment of conception, Mandela's parents hoped that he would cause change and or trouble in some way. This seems to suggest that from his birth, there was already a concept that Mandela would not be an ordinary member of the Thembu tribe, but that he would somehow change his environment. This is the kind of mentality Mandela was raised in throughout his childhood. He was raised to believe that he would not be a passive member of society, but that he would take action.[23]

Interpersonal Relations and Impact on Future Generations

Drawing from his background, Mandela's sense of family was very broad. He considered uncles, aunts, and cousins as fathers, mothers, brothers, and sisters. This was the approach of his culture, which in future years seemed to influence Mandela's broad view of his fellow Black South Africans and perhaps eventually the country itself, regardless of race. It seemed to reflect a generosity of spirit that, if nothing else, helped create conditions for cross-cultural discovery and coexistence.

On the other hand, and in large part due to his activism, Mandela's personal life suffered. Despite his apparent love for his children from two marriages, his wives, and those close to him, his intense ties to the anti-apartheid movement along with 27 years of imprisonment took their toll. Mandela reportedly experienced deep grief over these shortcomings and did his best to attend major family events. His children and his wives, however, appeared to resent the fact that Mandela was viewed as "father of the country" but much less so as father of his family.

In light of his collectivist sensibility, Mandela identified with the Zulu philosophy of "Ubuntu." This philosophy literally means "I am a person through other people. My humanity is tied to yours."[24] In a speech he delivered in 1997 at the Oxford Centre of Islamic Studies, Mandela stated: "The spirit of Ubuntu—that profound African sense that we are human only through the humanity of other human beings—is not a parochial phenomenon, but has added globally to our common search for a better world."[25]

In sum, family, culture, education, and worldview all seemed to coalesce as major influences on the life of Nelson Mandela. Although Mandela's background was very different from Frankl's and that of other resilient figures, there appeared to be many points of commonality, or at the least resonance. Among these commonalities are parents and surrogates with a larger view of life than conventional caretakers, a fierce determination to promote fairness and well-being in the world, a deep spiritual sensibility about one's life-path, a notable capacity to engage with people from a variety of backgrounds, and an interest in how such people live and what they live for. In all, and despite many personal struggles, Mandela's mark on humanity is vast. He is a touchstone for the courageous pursuit of social justice, but also dialogue across chasms of difference, and the grace, dignity, and appreciation of people becoming who they are through the encounter with other people.[26]

Overcoming Brokenness: Maya Angelou's Path to Wholeness (1928–2014)

Maya Angelou, who was born in St. Louis, Missouri, and died in Winston-Salem, North Carolina, was an extraordinarily accomplished writer, speaker, and public philosopher. In an influential television program hosted by Bill Moyers called "Facing Evil," Angelou described the key moments of her transformative past.[27] Beginning with her reference to the rape she experienced at seven years old, she went on to describe the guilt she experienced soon afterward when she heard that her rapist was killed. In her child's mind, she feared she caused his death. This profound guilt, along with the trauma of the rape, presumably prompted her to become mute for the next five years. As touched upon earlier, however, she began to undergo a transition during this period, largely from reading inspirational stories at her local library.

And when "I decided to speak," Angelou elaborated, "I had a lot to say, and many ways in which to say what I had to say it....Rape on the body of a young person," she went on, "more often than not introduces cynicism, and there is nothing quite so tragic as a young cynic, because it means going from knowing nothing to believing nothing." Yet, she countered, "out of this evil I was able to draw from human thought, human disappointments, and triumphs, enough to triumph myself."[28]

In addition to the healing she attained through books, she also describes an uncle who, despite many physical challenges, was pivotal on her healing path. "In a little Arkansas town," she recalls, "my uncle raised me. He was crippled. He left [his] town of Stamps, Arkansas, twice in his life.... He and my grandmother own the only Black-owned store in the town. He was obliged to work in the store, but he was severely crippled, so he needed me to help, and my brother."

So starting at age four, Angelou reflects,

> he started us to learn to read and write and do our times tables. In order to get me to do my times tables, he would take me behind my neck, grasp my clothes, and stand me in front of a pot-bellied stove. He would say, "Now sister, do your sixes." I did my sixes. I did my sevenses.... I was certain that because my uncle was crippled and strange looking that, had I not obeyed and obeyed quickly, he would have thrown me into the stove.[29]

Yet Angelou realized later that appearances are not necessarily reality and that her uncle was really quite a wise and caring fellow who "wouldn't let a moth be killed in [his] store." Many years later Angelou visited Stamps and found out that her Uncle Willie was a transformative figure for others in the town as well. She recounts the story of one man she met in the town by chance who mirrored her experience with her uncle.

"Because of your Uncle Willie," he said, "I'm who I am today. In the twenties, I was the only child of a blind mother. Your uncle gave me a job in [his] store, made me love to learn, and taught me times tables....I guess you want to know who I am today," the gentleman inquired of Angelou, and she nodded. "I'm Bussey. I'm the vice-mayor of Little Rock, Arkansas," he retorted.[30]

Angelou then goes on to describe another, younger man, who was mentored by Mr. Bussey, who "made [him] love to learn." And now he "was in the state legislature."[31]

"That which lives after us," Angelou observes and then pauses. "I look back at Uncle Willie," she continues, "crippled, Black, poor, unexposed to the world's great ideas—who left for our generation and generations to come a legacy so rich" that it moved her to write a poem titled "Willie"—that was later adopted by soul singer Roberta Flack.[32]

Angelou sums up her awe-based, vibrant-centered emergence as follows:

> If I admit, with Richard Wright in the poem "Between the World and Me that evil goes into me as does the good, then I'm obliged to study myself, to center myself and make a choice. For I must know the battles I wage are within myself. The wars I fight are in my mind. They are struggles to prevent the negative from overtaking the positive, and to prevent the good from eradicating all the negative and rendering me into an apathetic, useless organism, which has no struggle, no dynamic, and no life.[33]

Interpersonal Relations and Impact on Future Generations

Maya Angelou has been described as a goddess-like figure by those who knew her, like James Baldwin, Oprah Winfrey, and other friends and acquaintances. But, of course, like everyone else she had her vulnerabilities and limits. Lundi Ramsey Denfeld, a student of hers, summed up the force, presence, generosity, and principled fierceness of this remarkable woman:

> I met Maya Angelou back in 1980, while a student in Dolly McPherson's freshman English composition class at Wake Forest. This was before Dr. Angelou's affiliation with the university; Dr. McPherson had simply invited her friend to speak with us, a handful of young students. Corny as it sounds (I'm just gonna say it), I felt the air change when Maya Angelou entered the room. Her presence. Electric. Confusing. Exciting. Wondrous. She was a phenomenal woman (before I had even heard of, much less read [her poetry]); I needed no one to tell me she was a force, a bigger-than-life soul. The energy of Maya was just there, here, there. She spoke of her writing process; her habit of wearing only a large caftan with nothing else underneath which might inhibit or stifle her writing, the only other item on her body being a hat, with which to hold her thoughts in her head until she could put pen to paper, "I cannot let my thoughts escape," she smiled fiercely, broadly, raising her eyebrows and eyeing us individually....
>
> Dr. Angelou spoke of surrounding oneself with good people who are encouragers, and of not allowing others in one's presence to gossip or tear another human being down. She explained that at her many dinner parties, she never hesitated to abruptly stop conversation if she heard negativity, "Stop! I do not allow that type of talk at my table!" As I listened, I marveled. I wondered if it were possible for me to do this with friends, with acquaintances, without seeming rude. Obviously Dr. Angelou knew with a strength and a correct sense of rightness (not righteousness) what I did not, that it was a matter of who was the one actually being rude in this situation![34]

That said, Angelou took part in some of the most turbulent times in American history, with some of the most challenging personalities who led them. These times spanned the eras of

Jim Crow in the 1930s and 1940s and the Civil Rights movement in the 1960s and 1970s. Among the leaders she collaborated with were the previously mentioned James Baldwin, Nation of Islam leader Malcolm X, and Martin Luther King. Angelou's courage and principled nature were on full display during these difficult decades as well, as she became a dynamic activist who "spoke truth to power" and made concrete contributions not only to the African American community but the human community through her speeches, poetry, and teaching.

Angelou, whose three marriages ended in divorce, appeared to be a very devoted mother to her only son, the poet Guy Johnson. In an interview, just before Johnson died, he said:

> My mother's words often follow me, and they have to do with "pull up your sleaves, get ready for the struggle....life ain't no crystal staircase, you got to work and if you want a life for yourself, even as a paralyzed person [which Johnson was at the time] you got to get a grip on who you are. And it is with that that she allowed me to find a life, even when my body has forgotten me.
>
> She used to say, "can you imagine a world where every child was able to realize their potential and a life within [that potential]?... We would have the key to all the problems that set before us; but without that we can't do it. We need to get together. We need to see that each of us is part of the human family.[35]

In the end, Angelou left a breathtaking legacy of wonder at life, love for those close to her, and activism on behalf of a present, open, and discerning humanity.

Setting the Bar for Physical Resilience: Cosmologist Stephen Hawking (1942–2018)

The world-renowned cosmologist Stephen Hawking contracted the neurogenerative disease ALS at the tender age of 21. He was given two years to live. But in spite of this, he went on to live and achieve a stellar career for the next 55 years. There are, of course, no simple answers as to how this remarkable man picked up the pieces of his broken body and managed not only to survive but to thrive. To be sure, he had a rather privileged upbringing. His father was a medical researcher who graduated from the University of Oxford, and his mother, also a graduate of Oxford, obtained her degree in the Humanities. Hawking appears to have had a fairly happy childhood accompanied by a striking intellectual curiosity. Although he was an unexceptional student in primary and secondary school, he managed to blossom at Oxford and Cambridge, where he benefited from the mentorship of one of the great cosmologists in modern science, Roger Penrose, and cavorted, in his own right, with physics and the knotty perplexities of the universe. These engagements led—despite intensifying disability—to Hawking's appointment at the remarkable age of 35 to the professorial chair held by Isaac Newton at Cambridge University.[36]

Interpersonal Relations and Impact on Future Generations

As Hawking's illness worsened, he was unable to walk, write, or speak. He remedied this problem with adoption of a voice-activating machine that converted head and eye movements into words that were communicated through a synthetic voice. This technology opened vital avenues for Hawking to convey his research to very wide lay and professional audiences and to participate in forums that stimulated his trailblazing inquiries into the cosmos. Among these were fresh insights into the structure of black holes and origins of matter.

But what is most striking in the context of our focus here is Hawking's determination to pursue his passion for understanding the universe—as well as the human condition—despite and perhaps even in light of his ALS. For it was the onset of his ALS, according to his biography,[37] that spurred him into a much more present-centered and awe-based approach to life. Here's a quote from the comments Hawking delivered at the United Nations Sustainable Development Summit three years before he died that sums up much of the motivation for his pioneering life's work:

> I am very aware of the preciousness of time. Seize the moment. Act now.
>
> I have spent my life traveling across the universe inside my mind. Through Theoretical Physics I have sought to answer some of the great questions. But there are other challenges, other big questions which must be answered and these will also need a new generation who are interested, engaged, and with an understanding of science.
>
> One of the great revelations of the Space Age has been the perspective it has given humanity on ourselves. When we see the earth from space, we see ourselves as a whole. We see the unity and not the divisions. It is such a simple image with a compelling message. One planet. One human race.
>
> We are here together and we need to live together with tolerance and respect. We must become Global Citizens. Our only boundaries are the way we see ourselves. The only borders, the way we see each other.
>
> I have been enormously privileged through my work to be able to contribute to our understanding of the universe but it would be an empty universe indeed if it were not for the people I love and who love me. Without them the wonder of it all would be lost on me. Let us fight for every woman and every man to have the

> opportunity to live healthy, secure lives, full of opportunity and love.
>
> We are all time travelers, journeying together into the future. But let us work together to make that future a place we want to visit.
>
> Be brave, be determined, overcome the odds. It can be done.[38]

Hawking's resilience, like that of the luminaries discussed above, showed all the hallmarks of awe-based, vibrant-centered consciousness. For example, he was profoundly present. This presence was illustrated by his expanded consciousness following his ALS diagnosis, his ability to choose an attitude of wonder versus despair in the face of enormous difficulty, and his compassion for himself, others, and our planet. He was also radically open, as exemplified by his continual inquiries into the nature of existence and his remarkable capacity for innovation, both in his theoretical formulations and his treatment of his perplexing condition. Finally, Hawking showed great discernment about himself and others. He refused to short-change the opportunities he was afforded, and he disciplined himself into becoming a great scientist and respected public activist. In the end, and very much like Frankl, he showed that despite incalculable odds, a personally and socially gratifying life *can be achieved.*

A Light from Southeast Asia: Thich Nhat Hanh (1926–2022)

The Buddhist monk, peace activist, author, and teacher Thich Nhat Hanh was born in Hue, Vietnam and died in the same village at 95. Known as a socially engaged Buddhist, Nhat Hanh founded a school called the Plum Village Tradition to foster such practices and worked tirelessly to spread Buddhistic principles of mindfulness, equanimity, and social compassion throughout the world.

From early childhood, Nhat Hanh was exposed to political oppression and poverty due in large part to French rule over Vietnam. He learned to speak French, and his sizeable family, which was located in his grandmother's home, practiced French customs but also did their best to maintain their indigenous identity. His father was an official in the French administration of the family's district, and his mother was a homemaker. As he grew up, Nhat Hanh became increasingly sensitive to the plight of his people, especially the suffering of the poor and the growing divisions among classes. Due in part to some encounters he experienced at a young age—like an image of the Buddha, a meeting with a hermit, and an enchanted visit to a natural well—he deigned to become a Buddhist monk. At first his parents were skeptical of the idea, but eventually they supported him. Thus, at age 16 he began a path toward becoming a Buddhist monk, and at 23 he joined a monastery.

Dissatisfied with his monastic education, he pursued literature, philosophy, psychology, and science and received a degree in French and Vietnamese literature at Saigon University. He also sold books and poetry to support himself during this period. In the early 1960s, Nhat Hanh received a Fulbright scholarship to study comparative religion at Princeton and obtained a part-time teaching position at Columbia.[39]

Interpersonal Relations and Impact on Future Generations

Whatever combinations of disposition, talent, and life-experiences that impelled Nhat Hanh to become a deeply respected and widely known proponent of peace and the spiritually informed life is not all that evident. However, what is clear is that Nhat Hanh's development paralleled the development of many great influencers—displaying abounding curiosity, grit, persistence, empathy, and activism.[40] And we can add to this list creative transformation of his discipline. The latter is especially salient in his inspiration of "engaged" Buddhism. By engaged Buddhism, Nhat Hanh meant the active application of Buddhist principles to everyday life and to worldly affairs. With Nhat Hanh, Buddhism was no longer such a rarified practice, relegated to an elite community, but had the potential and, indeed, application to impact diverse people engaged in varied routines and lifestyles. His many travels and schools fostering engaged Buddhism brought these applications to life both in the East and West. Thus, one could observe Thich Nhat Hanh's influence on Martin Luther King and the struggles for civil rights and on the protests against the Vietnam War and the imperial designs of great powers in the East and West. When King nominated Nhat Hanh for the Nobel Peace Prize just prior to King's death in 1968, he wrote: "His ideas for peace, if applied would build a monument to ecumenism, to world brotherhood, to humanity."[41] The celebrated African American feminist writer bell hooks told Nhat Hanh when she first met him that she was "so angry." To which he reportedly replied, "Oh, hold on to your anger and use it as compost for your garden."[42] From then on, hooks intimated, her anger was thus transformed into a focus on love and, like King, she helped to broaden Nhat Hanh's message worldwide. She wrote of this period that:

> At last I had found a world where spirituality and politics could meet, where there was no separation. Indeed, in this world all efforts to end domination, to bring peace and justice, were spiritual practice. I was no longer torn between political struggle and spiritual practice. And here was the radical teacher—a Vietnamese monk living in exile—courageously declaring that "if you have to choose between Buddhism and peace, then you must choose peace."[43]

In his own words, Nhat Hanh pleads:

- “Don't make yourself into a battlefield; the world doesn't need any more fanatics." -from *Zen and the Art of Saving the Planet*
- "We all have the seeds of both anger and compassion." -from *Zen and the Art of Saving the Planet*
- “Without suffering, we do not have the opportunity to cultivate compassion and understanding; and without understanding, there can be no true love.” -from *You Are Here: Discovering the Magic of the Present Moment*
- "It is possible to listen to suffering in such a way that we don't get sucked in." -from *Zen and the Art of Saving the Planet*
- The most effective way to show compassion to another is to listen, rather than talk." -from *No Mud, No Lotus: The Art of Transforming Suffering*
- “If we believe that tomorrow will be better, we can bear a hardship today.” from *Peace Is Every Step: The Path of Mindfulness in Everyday Life*
- "You trust that you contain the whole cosmos; you are made of stars. And that is why you respect yourself and offer reverence to yourself. And, when you look at another person, you see that they are also made of stars. They are a wonderful manifestation. They don't appear only for a hundred years: they carry eternity within them." -from *Zen and the Art of Saving the Planet.*[44]

Feminist, Ethicist, and Humanitarian of France: Simone de Beauvoir (1908–1986)

Simone de Beauvoir was raised in an upper middle class Catholic family that suffered financial decline following World War I. De Beauvoir was purportedly a bright and spirited child who took seriously the contrasts and contradictions she experienced in her family and cultural life. For example, she witnessed her mother's traditional role as a housewife and the constraints of subordination and inequality that resulted. At the same time as she resented these outcomes and the patriarchy they implied, she was also greatly influenced by her father, a legal secretary, who stressed individuality and inquiry. De Beauvoir also had a crisis of faith at age 14. Primarily at her mother's insistence de Beauvoir was sent to a convent school, but she was so turned off by the restrictions on her identity as a female at the school that she rebelled and became intensely engaged with philosophy and existential questions about life.[45]

De Beauvoir also had a life-changing experience through her friendship with a peer named Zaza Lacoin. De Beauvoir perceived Lacoin as a model of free-spiritedness who related to de Beauvoir with equanimity and grace, a true friend who neither sought advantage from de Beauvoir nor insisted on equal investment in their relationship but was deeply caring and authentic. The two of them also had a rich intellectual relationship that in many ways formed the template for de Beauvoir's later masterwork *The Second Sex*.[46] Lacoin's mysterious death at the age of 21 was also foundation-shaking for de Beauvoir. In de Beauvoir's mind, in any case, Lacoin's death was associated with the oppression she suffered for being a liberated woman in an authoritarian world, which only deepened de Beauvoir's resolve to live freely and authentically.

De Beauvoir also appeared to be bisexual and had a series of relationships with women, aside from her over 50-year relationship with the famous existential philosopher Jean Paul Sartre. But de Beauvoir was not absolutist in her identifications with sexuality. What seemed most important for her was that the spiritual element of intimacy is intertwined with and foundational to the sexual dimension.[47]

Interpersonal Relations and Impact on Future Generations

De Beauvoir dedicated her life to supporting choice, freedom, and intersubjective or mutually respectful relationships, both between romantic partners and among cultures and society. She was an outspoken supporter of socialist and decolonial causes, and her book *The Ethics of Ambiguity* stresses the need for people to really grapple with their moral choices and not simply accept the received views. She argued that though all moral choices have elements of ambiguity, the "best" ones derive from deep consideration and attention to context (e.g., personal and circumstantial) rather than rote performance or ideological dogma.[48] In this, she shared sensibilities with Sartre's notion that we have great ranges of choice in our responses to events, and we neglect these choices at grave peril. This is the peril of turning ourselves into things as distinct from living, evolving human beings responsible for our world.

Here are some key themes directly from de Beauvoir's pen:

- [M]orality lies in the painfulness of an indefinite questioning.
- An action which wants to serve man ought to be careful not to forget him along the way...for the goal is not fixed once and for all; it is defined all along the road which leads to it. Vigilance alone can keep alive the validity of the goals and the genuine assertion of freedom.
- I am too intelligent, too demanding, and too resourceful for anyone to be able to take charge of me entirely. No one knows me or loves me completely. I have only myself.
- The lover describes her tears and her tortures, but she asserts that she loves this unhappiness. It is also a source of delight for her. She likes the other to appear as another through her separation. It pleases her to exalt, by her very suffering, that strange existence

which she chooses to set up as worthy of any sacrifice. It is only as something strange, forbidden, as something free, that the other is revealed as an other. And to love him genuinely is to love him in his otherness and in that freedom by which he escapes.

- [N]ihilistic pessimism and rationalistic optimism fail in their effort to juggle away the bitter truth of sacrifice: they also eliminate all reasons for wanting it.
- Ethics does not furnish recipes any more than do science and art. One can merely propose methods.[49]

As can be sensed, de Beauvoir lived her philosophy. The tension between apparent opposites such as good and bad, joy and discomfort, truth and uncertainty were ever the staging grounds for complex relations to self and other. But she didn't shy away from decision either; decision for de Beauvoir was a "leap of faith" as it was for Kierkegaard. But for de Beauvoir it was a present, openminded, and discerning leap, a leap that derived from grappling with and not merely reacting against the continual contraries—or "antinomies" as she called them—that beset us.

In sum, de Beauvoir left us a legacy of deep reflection on our subjective ability to make choices and shape our lives, but also at the same time our responsibility (or ability to respond) to the social challenges of our times. She appeared to be a devoted and loving friend, as in her relationship with Zaza Lecoin and other women she took under her wing, such as the philosophy professor Silvia Le Bon de Beauvoir, whom she literally "adopted" later in life. De Beauvoir and Le Bon were apparently intimate with each other for many years, and de Beauvoir took the radical step of "adopting" her so that so that she could legally oversee de Beauvoir's estate after she died. Le Bon reported being very grateful for the loving and caring connection she felt with De Beauvoir. Then there was de Beauvoir's 50-plus years with Jean Paul Sartre; although tumultuous at points, this relationship too involved very deep bonds, both personally and professionally. In all, de Beauvoir left us with an inspiring feminist—*and deeply human*—model for personal and collective fulfillment in this challenging age.

A Voice of Chinese Awakening: Lu Xun (1881–1936)

Lu Xun (pronounced "Looshoon") is one of the most underappreciated yet heroic figures in contemporary Chinese history. Lu Xun derived from an esteemed scholarly family in southeastern China. Despite this, he labored under some very difficult circumstances, including the death of his chronically ill father when Lu Xun was a young teenager. During this period, from about ages 14–16, Lu Xun went to great lengths to help his ailing father. He pawned his family's wealthy possessions and used the money to purchase all manner of "unusual drugs" from purportedly "quack" doctors of Chinese medicine.[50] This episode was very disillusioning for Lu Xun as his father went from "bad to worse" after taking the drugs, and it brought into light a budding skepticism about certain practices touted as superlative in his country but that ended up causing more harm than good.[51]

Another parallel event that significantly impacted Lu Xun's growing philosophy of life was the indictment and subsequent imprisonment of his grandfather, who was a high-ranking official in the Chinese government. The indictment was for fraud and precipitated the downfall of Lu Xun's privileged family status. This incident and its consequent effects reinforced the young Lu Xun's evolving skepticism about political authority and the dubiousness of appearances.[52]

On the positive side of his family life, Lu Xun was supported to pursue classical Chinese literature and history. Yet after his family's financial difficulties, he decided to leave his hometown and study Western culture and technology at a more "affordable" university. This was a very risky move, however, because the message he received from his community was that in his words: "Anyone who studied 'foreign' subjects was a social outcast" and they were "regarded as someone who could find no way out and forced to sell his soul to foreign devils." But in contrast, Lu Xun's action signaled an authenticity that opened himself to new "paths" and "novel places, while searching for a new breed of people with different characteristics—a new personality." Lu Xun thus went on to "study physics, arithmetic, geography, history, drawing, and physical training" at a Nanjing Navel Academy. He "opened his mind" and began to take in "the influence of foreign culture." In time, Lu Xun began to read such icons of Western literature as "Huxley, Socrates, Plato, Tolstoy, and Nietzsche," the latter of whom became particularly influential later in Lu Xun's life.

Lu Xun then went on to study Western medicine in Japan and became a kind of physician–philosopher. His overriding aim was to help his fellow Chinese to rise up and avoid the kind of fates he had witnessed in the lives of both his grandfather and father. He asked questions like "What is the ideal human character? What is most lacking in the Chinese character? What is the root cause of the problem?"[53] One of the chief maladies Lu Xun saw in the Chinese population at the time was apathy, a sense of helpless compliance with outside powers. This was a time when Russia was at war with China,, and the Opium wars with Great Britain were not that distant. There seemed to be a complacency among the Chinese people, according to Lu Xun, that began to inspire him to speak out and write publicly to address the matter. He thus initiated a magazine called *New Life* to pursue his vision, but this failed miserably and dropped him into a state of notable despair. He struggled with this despair, which he equated with a "poisonous snake," and battled with his "strong desire for meaning" at the same time as his skeptical attitude toward life."[54] Ultimately, Lu Xun began to emerge from this turmoil by facing both his abounding despair and his growing recognition that life, even at its most poignant, contained both despair and possibility. He learned, especially from Nietzsche to say "yes" to life in spite of and even alongside its many negatives. In fact, he saw how the so-called negatives were also gateways to a larger and enriching existence.

Later in the 1930s, Lu Xun joined the liberal Chinese leader Sun Yat-sen's widow, Soon Quingling, in organizations such as the China League of Civil Rights to oppose fascism and imperialism. In a genuine sense, Lu Xun took up "pen warfare" in his mission to fight passivity, complacency, and the coercive politics that too often result.[55]

One of Lu Xun's most powerful works was his allegory of *The Iron House*.[56] Symbolically speaking, this is the story of Lu Xun standing before an iron house where the inmates are all sound asleep. The house has no obvious windows or doors and the inmates are in peril of dying. Thus, Lu Xun is faced with a monumental dilemma. Should he bang on the wall of the house and wake the inmates up in the hope—however slim—that they might find a way to free themselves? Or should he ignore their peril and seal their fate to a passive yet certain demise? Again, symbolically speaking, this tale reflects Lu Xun's anxiety about his own life, such as the time he attempted to save his father's life but was faced with useless medicines and an irritable demeanor from his father, who asked Lu Xun not to bother saving him. The story also parallels Lu Xun's dilemma with the Chinese people of his time, whom he felt were paralyzed in slumber but resistant to waking up and risking change. The risks actually went both ways—the risk of imminent death if Lu Xun failed to awaken the slumbering inmates in the story (by implication the society) and the risk of terrifying those inmates (by implication citizens of China) if he awakens them and they find there is no solution to their plight. It appears that Lu Xun leaned toward the side of waking people up despite and in light of the slim odds.

Lu Xun wrote many similar allegories about the risks of activism and liberation. He welded the confrontational element of Nietzsche with the balanced and harmonizing vision of Confucius. In so doing, he showed how a blend of these two converged on the enlargement of awareness (presence). This presence inspired people to rediscover their sense of aliveness, authenticity; while also alerting them to their responsibilities for the collective.

Interpersonal Relations and Impact on Future Generations

Lu Xun had two marriages. The first was apparently arranged by his parents and saddled him from the traditional standpoint of filial piety and financial support rather than romance. His second marriage, however, was reported to be much warmer and more intimate. It was a "loving modern marriage" with one of his students that produced two sons, with whom he was "patient, considerate, and loving." As Manfield Zhu elaborated:

> Lu Xun and Xu Guangping [his second wife] had worked and lived along together for 13 years until he passed away on October 19, 1936. The couple had loved each other, helped each other and learnt from each other, which was one of the most important reasons that Lu Xun had great contributions to China and all over the world.
>
> People used to think that Lu Xun was a hard-boned man. He never stopped sharpening his pen and he was so dauntless and unyielding to expose and reveal all the enemies' ugly manners. His pen was mightier than any sword holding in his opponents and foes. As his serious disease [progressed] he had no time enough to complete what he wanted to do or write, he left a piece of paper entitled Death. "As I got fever, [I was reminded] of the European ceremonies before one is going to die, [in] which the dying man will be asked to forgive the other(s) or to be forgiven by the other(s). How many opponents and foes I have! If I were asked the same question, what would I like to answer? I think

> over it for a little while, I decide to answer: Let them hate me forever, but no one will be forgiven."
>
> Lu Xun had not compromised with any enemy. However, his heart was not like a stone; his mind was full of love. He loved all the common people with good intentions, but at the same time, he would like to point out their shortcomings in detail in his articles. Lu Xun's love and hate were clearly demarcated.[57]

Ultimately, Lu Xun left a deep mark, personally, politically, and spiritually, on his society. He developed the idea of "Zhi Mian," which means "*directly facing reality*. He championed the zhi mian warrior, as the one who," in Lu Xun's words, "dares to face life as it is, no matter how gloomy it might be."[58] Like Frankl and Nietzsche before him, Lu Xun stressed that though we cannot always change external circumstances, we can in our own way respond creatively to them, and live the meaningful life.

A Voice of Arab Humanism: Edward Said (1935–2003)

Edward Said faced a powerful array of cultural and political forces from the beginning of his life. He was born in Jerusalem to a wealthy Protestant family and to a father who was a businessman and American citizen. Early on he learned to speak English and French. Though Arabic was discouraged at home, he was intimately exposed to it—as well as to Islam—growing up in both pre-Israel Palestine and, later, in his teenage years in Cairo, Egypt. This latter period was instigated by what his fellow Palestinian neighbors called the Nakba or "catastrophe," when the British Colonial government granted the Jewish population of Palestine a territory of their own called the State of Israel.[59]

After attending a series of British schools in both Jerusalem and Cairo, Said was sent to Northfield Mount Hermon School in Massachusetts at age 16. There he flourished academically but also felt isolated and was treated as an outsider.

Said's life was a trying blend of Middle Eastern and Western languages, cultures, and communities. He was exposed early to a worldly experience of diversity and education but also the estrangement and degradation that attended it. These were tumultuous times of colonial and post-colonial transition, Israeli–Palestinian clashes, and the growing tension between aggressive Western cultural and economic policies and Arab resistance to those policies, with Said dwelling at their crux.[60]

However, far from being a passive bystander to these upheavals, Said was a battler himself. In particular, he transformed his personal and collective experiences into a springboard for activism. He distinguished himself as a leading academic and public philosopher who advocated for a complex humanism. For example, in his major work *Orientalism*, Said made an impassioned plea for a more nuanced approach to Arabic culture.[61] Through their stereotypic portrayals, he asserted, the Western powers generally, and the United States in particular, persistently dehumanized Arabic ways of life. As Hibri put it, Said showed:

> how Orientalist writings and ideologies actively shape the world they describe, and how they perpetuate views of Middle Eastern people as inferior, subservient, and in need of saving. As a result, these often racist or romanticized stereotypes create a worldview that justifies Western colonialism and imperialism.[62]

On the other hand, Said also challenged the mounting bigotry of extremists in the Middle East and reserved some of his harshest criticism for Islamic fundamentalism. He contended that these groups, albeit instigated in many cases by the Orientalist degradations of the West, were nevertheless reckless in their own right by fomenting violence and dehumanization toward populations in the West. Thus, Said advocated for a dynamically centered position that opposed both the colonizing mentality of the West and the reactionary mentality of some of those who were colonized.[63] In sum, Said supported a humanism that "centered upon the agency of human individuality and subjective intuition, rather than on received ideas and approved authority. Texts have to be read as texts that were produced and live on in the historical realm in all sorts of what I have called worldly ways."[64]

Ultimately, Said can be seen as a voice for the vibrantly centered, culturally attuned individual in a world of skewed and reactive ideologues. Although Said was Christian by birth, he was intimately identified with Arabic culture, and he became a champion of humanizing that culture. But he also became a champion of humanizing Western culture. He stood in that rare position of feeling rooted in a tribe, a rich history, and a righteous outrage, while also opening up to other tribes' rich histories and righteous outrages. He showed that one can be fiercely aligned with oppressed communities but also make independent choices about other alignments and sympathies. He grew up in a hotbed of religious sensibilities, but he wound up in a fervor of secular interests and critiques. He understood traditional dress, ritual, but he also related to the dynamism of the academy and the free-thinking of liberal democracies. Deeply cultural and multicultural at the same time, Said gave us insights into a potentially creative future, a future that enables a sense of deep belonging, whether to a tribe, a family, or a lover. But he also gave us a path to unknown worlds, new adaptations, and fresh connections. This is the path of wonder and discovery alongside some degree of rootedness, comfort in one's own skin and the skin of one's heritage.

Interpersonal Relations and Impact on Future Generations

Overall, Said appears to have been an involved and caring parent and husband. This overview, however, is complicated by reports that during his second marriage, he had an affair with another woman. He also apparently could be quite prickly with colleagues who disappointed or challenged him. Yet he also displayed great generosity and support for many who sought his counsel. His love of music also had a tempering effect on him. This was exemplified by his collaboration with the prominent Israeli conductor Daniel Berenboim to create an Israeli–Palestinian orchestra called the "West–Eastern Divan Orchestra." Jews and Arabs playing Beethoven, he intimated, canceled out their differences. From Said's standpoint, they created beauty together, and that was the essence of the project.[65]

Said was apparently very supportive of his son and daughter. He was reported to have been overjoyed at the prospect of his son Wadi's marriage, and he was a notable influence on his daughter, Najla, who became an accomplished author, actor, and activist. In an interview several years after her father's death, Najla remarked that being with her father and meeting the many thoughtful and creative people he knew was pivotal for her development. She also noted that, like many who made contact with him, she harbored a reverential feeling for him. At the same time, she acknowledged that she grew up in his shadow in many instances, which was partly her impetus for choosing a distinctive career path in her own right.[66]

There is little doubt that Said's works, particularly on Orientalism, but also his meetings with political leaders, such as Yasser Arafat in 1974 and U.S. Secretary of State George Shultz in 1988, had a significant impact on society at large. In these public arenas, Said was consistent; he made great efforts to address the urgency of a Palestinian homeland, while at the same time appealing to Palestinians (and other Arabs) to officially recognize the State of Israel.[67] Said's stances on behalf of Palestinians and the Arabic world, combined with his humanistic vision for peaceful coexistence, continues to inspire many, particularly in secular and more moderate religious circles, to carry his message forward. Although in the wake of the October 7, 2023 Palestinian attack on Israel and its devastating consequences, Said's social ideals have been badly tarnished, his legacy of holding and encountering cultural and political differences remains an elevating aspiration.

Soul and Humanism from Spain: Federico Lorca (1898–1936)

Federico Garcia Lorca, one of the great Spanish poets of the 20th century, was assassinated by vengeful nationalists in 1936 at the dawn of the Spanish civil war. Lorca is perhaps best known for his poetry, but he was also a musician, a playwright, and a theater director. Although Lorca had Leftist leanings, and he despised fascism as well as bourgeois aristocracy, he refused to join a political party, preferring instead to express his activism through his art.

A headstrong child, Lorca grew up in a wealthy family in a village outside of the Spanish city of Granada. Lorca's father was a successful landowner and his mother a teacher. Despite a complex relationship, Lorca's father reportedly loved and supported Lorca, even when he disagreed with him, and his mother taught him the great value of education and reading classics, which he began at age four. Lorca also suffered from a serious illness that prevented him from walking until age four. This illness however had the catalyzing effect of increasing Lorca's "powers of imagination" in the absence of his ability to join other children at play.[68] As a result, Lorca learned to play on his own and created his own "theaters, marionettes, processions."[69] He also dressed up his servants and other members of his family and began to create his own plays. He lived in the countryside and began to learn Andalusian folktales—romances and ballads—from the old servants around him as well as from elders in the surrounding town. He apparently relished these influences along with the lush landscape that also connected him with ancient sensibilities.

From these roots, Lorca resonated with Spanish folklore, including Andalusian Flamenco (a style of dance), and Gypsy culture, each of which is evident in his lyrics. Echoing these lineages, he embraced what may be called "deep song" whose notable historical roots feature the poignancy of romance against the backdrop of tragedy and death. Lorca himself was reportedly gay and had several ill-fated affairs. At the same time, some of the people he courted, such as Salvador Dali, opened doors for him in the salons of Spain. During his time in Madrid, for example, Lorca not only became friends with Dali but also with the great filmmaker Luis Bunuel, along with other visual artists and poets. The avant garde movement of Surrealism also significantly influenced Lorca's work. Later, and with the support of artists and academics in Madrid, Lorca spent time studying at Columbia University in New York. But as with his time at universities in Granada and Madrid, he was more interested in experiencing life than studying about it, although clearly his education impacted his ability to think, write, and conceptualize.[70]

One of the essential themes to emerge from Lorca's writing and feeling about art is his concept of "duende." Duende is an intense mysterious force that wells up from the depths of the artist's creation—whether in song, dance, poetry, or other creative forms. It is an ancient sensibility that appears connected to Flamenco dance in its connection to the earth, darkness, and death but also and equally to aliveness, vibrance, and sensuality. It is a joyous affirmation of the moment against the background of fragility and decay, a cry of love, risk, and adventure against the starkness of limits.[71]

Like many artistic modes, duende combines form and vitality, as Rollo May put it; or to state it another way: the capacity to move within constraints, the beauty of vibrancy within mystery.[72] Here's one of Lorca's most famous passages about duende. Echoing the Flamenco singer Manuel Torres, Lorca wrote:

> "All that has dark sounds has *duende*." And there is no greater truth.
>
> These "dark sounds" are the mystery, the roots, thrusting into the fertile loam, known to all of us, ignored by all of us, but from which we get real art....
>
> Thus the *duende* is a power not a behaviour; it is a struggle, not a concept. I have heard an old guitarist master say: "The *duende* is not in the throat; the *duende* surges up from the soles of the feet." Which means it is not a matter of ability, but of real live form; of blood of ancient culture; of creative action.
>
> This "mysterious power that everyone feels but that no philosopher has explained" is in fact the spirit of the earth....

Lorca concludes:

> All in the Arts are capable of possessing *duende*, but naturally the field is widest in music, in dance, and in spoken poetry, because they require a living body as interpreter—they are forms that live and die ceaselessly, and are defined by an exact present.[73]

Interpersonal Relations and Impact on Future Generations

According to several accounts, Lorca had a lively, gregarious personality and loved life with friends and fellow artists, particularly in cafés and country meadows. In all frankness, he seemed to enjoy this informal life more than academia, despite having come into contact with some of the great thinkers in history there. For example, while studying at the Residentia de Estudiantes in Madrid, he was exposed to philosophers such as Henri Bergson and Ortega Y Gassett and writers such as G.K.

Chesterton and H.G. Wells.[74] At the same time, and despite or perhaps in light of being openly gay, Lorca struggled with romantic relationships. They tended to be transient and when at least one of them was over, he lapsed into a marked depression.[75] That said, Lorca appeared to have a rich and meaningful bond with many friends, mentors, and fellow artists. His rootedness in nature and the ancient Andalusian culture, which was a rich admixture of Arabic and Western influences, appeared to deepen his affirmation of life and the whole-bodied experiences that attend.

Lorca's concept of duende in particular has made its mark across many decades, and seemed to symbolize both his humanistic ideal as well as his critique of modern consumerist society. He aspired to reconnect people with their primal experience of nature, while at the same time encouraging their free-thinking and creativity. Given that these qualities represented a threat to the fascist–militarist powers of his day as well as to the industrialists, he paid, it appears, with his life. He also paid dearly for his homosexuality and his openness to alternative lifestyles. And yet, Lorca experienced and portrayed to others what a rich and full life could look like. This was a life of experimentation and some wildness, to be sure, but also one of sensitivity to the plight of others, enlivening and transcendent artistry, and the belief that if mindfully *interpreted,* the life-force of duende is available to all.

A Social Conscience from East Europe: Andrei Tarkovsky (1932–1986)

Andrei Arsenyevich Tarkovsky was arguably the greatest film director of his generation. This is what the iconic Ingmar Bergman suggested in interviews and on book covers.[76] Through films like *Andrei Rublev* (1966), *Solaris* (1972), *The Mirror* (1975), *Stalker* (1979), and *The Sacrifice* (1986), Tarkovsky explored the tension between human vulnerability and the need for structure, technology and spirituality, and estrangement and awe-based connection. Despite years of struggle as a Russian artist under Soviet rule, he found ways to create films that challenged the system and, by implication, all authoritarian systems that squelched creativity and stifled personal inquiry. He embraced religion albeit not as a tranquilizer but as a sensibility critical to the nihilistic age. This sensibility celebrated questions as much as faith and cradled his Eastern Orthodox roots as much as the multifaceted roots of other faiths such as Zen Buddhism, Taoism, mysticism, and humanism.[77] In *Solaris*, a precursor of *2001: A Space Odyssey*, Tarkovsky explores the mystery of outer (and inner) space and the too often futile quest of science to explain this puzzlement. On the face of it, the film focuses on a state-sponsored effort to rescue a crew of astronauts who became lost on a far away planet called "Solaris." Attending the rescue mission are some very seasoned pilots, military officers, and investigators. However, the film highlights one astronaut in particular, a psychologist who relies heavily on cognitive–behavioral—that is, strictly rational—principles to both understand the mission and "treat" the victims once they are found. However, this worldview soon proves inadequate, and as the mission proceeds closer to its destination, the psychologist undergoes what might be called a psycho-spiritual conversion. Once the rescue ship arrives near the planet's surface, strange sights, sounds, and movements begin to emerge. There are prominent cutaways to undulating weeds in a vast sea, and disturbing dreams and visions begin to affect the crew, including the psychologist. At one point as they hover over the planet's surface with no sign of their lost compatriots, the psychologist begins to wax philosophical with another senior officer about the mysteries not only of their particular mission but of existence itself. This is one of the most eloquent and absorbing sequences in the film. Here is a little sample: The psychologist states, "To ask is always the desire to know. Yet the preservation of simple human truths requires mystery. The mysteries of happiness, death, and love. To think about it is to know one's day of death." The other officer replies, "Maybe you're right, but try not to think about all that now." The psychologist (seemingly acknowledging the other officer's avoidance of the question) responds, "Not knowing that day makes us practically immortal."[78]

After many years of tangling with the Soviet authorities, Tarkovsky spent the last year of his all-too-brief life in exile in Paris. He completed his final film, *The Sacrifice,* shortly before he succumbed to cancer in 1986.

Interpersonal Relations and Impact on Future Generations

Tarkovsky had a troubled and yet enlivening past. His father, a famous Russian poet, reportedly separated from Tarkovsky's mother when Tarkovsky was three, and abandoned the family for service in World War II when Tarkovsky was ten. Ironically Tarkovsky himself repeated a similar cycle with his son, separating from his wife when his son was three and leaving to start a new family when his son was eight. Nevertheless, Tarkovsky was apparently deeply influenced and inspired by his father's poetry, and his films reflect that poetic sensibility. Tarkovsky was largely raised by his mother, who also encouraged his artistic nature despite his rebelliousness at an early age. Tarkovsky's loving yet complex relationship with his mother is poignantly depicted in his 1975 film *The Mirror.*

Overall, Tarkovsky was a passionate, deeply spiritual and sometimes demanding and abrasive filmmaker. He influenced many directors of his generation such as Bergman, along with more contemporary directors such as Stephen Soderberg and Lars von Trier. He also inspired his son Andrey to become a prominent director in his own right. Tarkovsky had several marriages, but his last one seemed to be the most stable and enduring.[79]

Despite his personal and professional challenges, Tarkovsky left us a legacy of keen insight and prophetic vision.

He delved into the heart of human pathos as well as creativity and transcendence. His own words, which speak for themselves, are a rallying cry for art, the vibrant center of life, and awe-based consciousness:

> ...the goal for all art—unless of course it is aimed at the "consumer," like a saleable commodity—is to explain to the artist himself and to those around him what [humanity] lives for, what is the meaning of [our] existence. To explain to people the reason for their appearance on this planet; or if not to explain, at least to pose the question....
>
> Through the image is sustained an awareness of the infinite; the eternal within the finite; the spiritual within matter; the limitless given form.[80]

On the matter of social conscience, he writes:

> If a person's sense of responsibility for the future of society is not based on an inner conviction of the part he has to play, if he merely feels entitled to make use of other people, directing their inner lives for them and indoctrinating them with the idea of their role in the development of society, then the discord between the individual and society can only become more bitter.... Freedom is not something that can be incorporated into a [person's] life once and for all: it has to be constantly achieved through moral exertion. In relation to the outside world [a person] is essentially unfree because [they] are not alone; but inner freedom [they have] from the start, if only [they] can summon the courage and resolution to use it, accepting that [their] *inner* experience is of *social* significance.[81]

Other Carriers of Awe-Based, Vibrantly Centered Consciousness

The luminaries described above are but a carefully chosen snapshot of resilient lives across our variously broken families, communities, and societies throughout our world. But we would be remiss if we failed to mention at least a portion of the other luminaries who shared similar paths to those above, and who likewise pave the way for an awe-based, vibrantly centered consciousness. Among these are Mohandas Gandhi, who centered himself in nonviolent protest and interfaith cooperation; Martin Luther King, who also centered himself in nonviolent protest and interfaith collaboration but additionally addressed the psychological dimensions underlying prejudice and injustice; Dolores Huerta and Caesar Chavez,[82] who bravely transformed their impoverished backgrounds in the service of nonviolently supporting the rights of their fellow farmworkers; Dorothy Day, who tirelessly supported the rights of women and the working class but found a vibrant center between Catholic dogma, passivity, communist atheism, and revolutionary aggression; Albert Camus, who stood for a vibrant middle between Communist collectivism and capitalist individualism, violent rebellion, and compliant passivism; and Eleanor Roosevelt, who passionately advocated for the empowerment of women and individual responsibility within a caring, compassionate collective. There are many others who could be added to this list such as 13th century Sufi poet and mystic Jalāl al-Dīn Muḥammad Rūmī, 18th century German philosopher and statesman Johann Wolfgang von Goethe, 19th century Danish philosopher and originator of existentialism Soren Kierkegaard, 19th and 20th century American psychologist and public philosopher William James, 20th century German philosopher and conceiver of the "I–Thou" relationship Martin Buber, 20th century German theologian and public philosopher Paul Tillich, 20th century Greek author and public philosopher

Nikos Kazantzakis, 20th century Japanese filmmaker Akira Kurosawa, 20th century American author and political essayist James Baldwin, and countless allied trailblazers. However, the chief point here is that collectively, these are extraordinary people who dared to stretch beyond the borders of simplistic answers and knee jerk reactions. They seized life from a strong central vantage point, which organically and sometimes painstakingly led to pauseful, reflective, and deeply meaningful ventures.

What Have We Learned About Awe-Based, Vibrantly Centered Consciousness?

We have now seen how both everyday people, as well as historical luminaries, have mustered the grit, creativity, and resilience it takes to engage in a vibrantly centered life. The chief question, of course, is how do we seed our society and indeed world to exemplify that kind of liveliness, resolve, and motivation? This is a question we will turn to momentarily. For now, however, we need to explore a more preliminary question: What are the qualities that the people we have surveyed share and offer to the world?

First and foremost, our sample underscores the value of an enriching background, and if not enriching economically, then enriching in terms of both the human and environmental resources that elevated and transformed the subjects' lives. Accordingly, the engagement with *surrogates, mentors,* or *inspirational ventures* was critical for subjects in developing vibrant centered lives. The availability of books, schools, cultural rituals, and free-thinking political circumstances were also integral. Or, to put it in the context of this book's thesis, human and environmental resources inspired the cultivation of presence, openness, and discernment. It spurred our extraordinary sample to clarify the meaning and direction of their lives, and these qualities, in turn, led to the inspiration of many others, the liberation of many others, to pursue kindred paths.

The second common quality among our sample is the *embrace of the contrasts and contradictions of living—the paradoxes of living*. From their position of dynamic centeredness, these exemplary folks developed an ability to confront and grapple with uncomfortable thoughts, feelings, body sensations, and intuitions about life. They learned to work with these discomforts despite their primal echoes of fear of the unknown, the radically different, and the unpredictable. Instead of being daunted by these otherwise distressing sides of life, most of our sample seemed energized by them—at least comparatively speaking. They felt called to reflect on them, explore them, and integrate them into projects for both themselves and their fellow human beings. The projects took the form of life-philosophies, artistic creations, ethical stances, and scientific discoveries. They also took the form of down-to-earth contributions to family, community well-being, and the health and welfare of our world.

The third common quality among the exemplars is their *capacity for authenticity*; their capacity to draw from their own center of meaning, even if that center was informed primarily by communal or spiritual influences. The issue is whether the meaning was notably intentional, mindful, and vital *to that particular person*. And the answer in all cases, whether communally oriented or individually leaning, was a resounding "yes!"

A fourth commonality is the emphasis on *worldliness*. These exemplars tended to live wide-ranging lives, traveling to distant lands, becoming acquainted with diverse cultures, and integrating varieties of experience. This worldliness was also based on *courage*—courage to take risks, courage to not just think about but actively encounter differences. Where did the courage come from? It came from an enriching environment, or at least from enriching and encouraging people and places in that environment. And it came from grit, or the determination to overcome barriers to a fuller and more engaged life, which leads to the sixth commonality—*persistence.*

The extraordinary sample we surveyed were all *persistent, hard workers.* There is a myth that sometimes circulates about successful people being lazy, soft, and lucky. But this is far from the case for the successful people surveyed above. They all showed a great willingness to exert themselves, to pursue their artistic, philosophical, poetic, scientific or political project to maximal degrees. They refused to take "no" for an answer—whether that rebuff came from parents, friends, civic authorities, or even their own medical conditions. They found ways around those hurdles and carried on with their causes. They were passionate to live life as fully as possible, not only perhaps because they had some biological propensities to do so but mainly, I would contend, because they had the strength of character based on all the other commonalities—enriched environments, the encounter with life's paradoxes, the insistence on authenticity, worldliness, and courage—to see their work through.

In sum, each of those surveyed developed extraordinary presence, openness to experience, and discernment in their life-causes and engagement with their larger social worlds. They inspired others, in some cases multitudes, to pursue similar paths and pave the way for their successors to follow suit. The question is, are we now at a point where these influences do not merely reside at the margins of societal functioning but course into its very heart? What resources do we have at our disposal now that can facilitate this vibrancy, and how do they work? This is what we will turn to presently with a fuller description of one such previously noted, resource, The Corps of Depth Healers Certificate Program.[83]

One Grass-Roots Effort to Seed an Awe-Based, Vibrantly Centered Society: The Corps of Depth Healers Certificate Program

I am not naïve enough to think that the Corps of Depth Healers (CODH) Certificate Program that I co-founded with my colleague Tyler Gamlen is a sure bet to transform our polarized and awe-depleted world. But I am concerned enough to propose it as a pilot effort to nudge our society toward a more life-affirming direction.

The premise of the Corps is that until vibrant-centered, awe-based lives are prioritized by our socioeconomic systems and government, the private sector needs to take action on them and mobilize itself. This mobilization needs to be modeled on the resiliency of people like our survey sample and foster conditions of enriching environments, encounters with life's paradoxes, authenticity, worldliness, and courage in order for substantive change to occur. In our view at the Corps, *emotionally restorative relationships,* or relationships where people feel heard and seen and that get at the roots of their problems, are essential for such substantive change to occur. In other words, the Corps provides one example, one pilot effort to organize a movement of societal healers to hone their skills and extend emotionally restorative relationships as far and wide as possible, throughout our country and world. Now, it is important to underscore that this movement is not seeking to impose emotionally restorative relationships on people but to *make them available* at affordable, accessible rates. This is a peoples' project—in other words, a grass-roots effort to transfer depth principles of practice from the "towers" of academia and sacred societies to everyday lives. By "depth principles of practice," we mean approaches that emphasize emotionally restorative relationships, implicit as well as explicit elements of interaction, and comparatively intimate relationships—distinct from simplistic or formulaic "fixes."

To set the example of "giving away" this knowledge, we have structured the online CODH Certificate Program as a free, wide-ranging endeavor.[84] It is a "big tent" movement that enables eligibility for anyone who has graduated from a regionally accredited program with a bachelor's degree in a helping profession to apply. This population includes but is not limited to psychologists, psychiatrists, social workers, counselors, educators, nurse practitioners, physicians, clergy, home care workers, and hospital aides. Upon acceptance into the program, enrollees take a 10-week curated curriculum consisting of Section 1—a two-week Introduction and Overview, and Section 2—an eight-week segment of articles and videos that provide skill-building in eleven possible areas of Emphasis (or specialties). The Section 2 Emphases are:

1. Bridge-Building Dialogues
2. Depth-Oriented Social Work and Family Systems
3. Depth-Oriented Spiritual Care
4. Depth-Oriented Psychotherapy for Underserved Communities
5. Depth-Oriented Medical Care
6. Awe-Based Environmental Psychology
7. Relational Approaches to Social Justice
8. Life Coaching and Mentoring for Underserved Populations
9. Humanistic and Awe-Based Education
10. Humanistic Approaches to Management and Diplomacy
11. Depth-Oriented School Counseling

Enrollees are asked to choose one area of emphasis for their engagement in the balance of the course. They also have full access to a curated library rich with articles and videos that include but also exceed the assigned resources for each of the emphases. The library also houses recordings of the video consults, which are provided at the start, middle, and end of the course and offer opportunities for cohorts to interact with each other and share questions or concerns with the program creators (Tyler and me) in a "Town Hall" format. The consults also include a "graduation" component in which enrollees share their "case studies," which are very brief concluding essays outlining what enrollees learned from the course and how they plan to apply it to their practices or services in their communities. The recordings are not meant to be substitutes for live engagement in the video consults but generators of ideas, observations, and directions that may help enrollees improve their experiences of the consults and refine their final case studies.

Finally, enrollees have access to the "Depth Dialogues" podcast series. This is an interview series conducted by Tyler and me with leaders from a range of depth-oriented fields that are also represented in the Certificate Program and that are dedicated to social healing. As a last step, enrollees who complete the program receive a certificate identifying them as having completed the course in societal Depth Healing.

To provide a more detailed overview, here are a couple of examples of the structure of the CODH Certificate Program. The first is an excerpt from Section 1, the introduction to and overview of the program, and the second is a sample of two modules from Section 2, the Emphases portion:[85]

Section I: Core Principles of Social Healing, Part I: Theoretical Foundations

1. Introduction: The Need for Emotionally Restorative Relationships
2. Essential Frameworks for Emotional Restoration in Social Healing
3. Philosophical and Psychological Foundations of Social Healing
4. Relational and Emotional Foundations of Social Healing
5. Cultural and Societal Foundations of Social Healing

6. Spiritual and Existential Foundations of Social Healing
7. Political and Systemic Dimensions of Social Healing
8. Community-Based Foundations of Social Healing
9. Conclusion: Toward a Model of Depth Psychology for Social Healing

Introduction: The Need for Emotionally Restorative Relationships

In an era of profound sociopolitical polarization, existential anxiety, and increasing psychological distress, there is a pressing need for emotionally restorative relationships. Traditional approaches to healing often focus on symptom reduction rather than addressing the deeper existential wounds that shape an individual's experience of suffering. Depth psychology, rooted in existential–phenomenological, psychodynamic, and humanistic traditions, offers a framework for social healing that extends beyond the individual to encompass relational, cultural, and systemic transformation. This section explores philosophical and psychological foundations of social healing, drawing upon major thinkers such as Martin Buber, Erich Fromm, Frantz Fanon, Kirk Schneider, Carl Rogers, Rollo May, Simone Weil, and others. By integrating existential thought, psychoanalytic insights, and humanistic principles, depth psychology provides a path toward authentic healing in which individuals are truly seen and heard, not merely treated or managed.

The "Corps of Depth Healers Certificate Program" is designed to provide an opportunity to deepen the learner's knowledge of the various psychological, cultural, spiritual, and societal factors that influence individual and collective healing. Drawing upon depth psychology, the program acknowledges the deep-rooted connections between personal and collective trauma while also exploring the tools and strategies necessary to facilitate healing at all levels. The following sections outline the key foundations that inform the program's framework, setting the stage for a comprehensive and holistic approach to social healing.

Now here are two examples from Section 2 of the Emphases, beginning with module 1, Bridge Building Dialogues:

Bridge Building Dialogues
Course Description

In a time marked by cultural fragmentation, political hostility, and widespread disconnection, the Bridge Building Dialogues' emphasis prepares students to facilitate conversations that cultivate empathy, relational depth, and civic healing. Grounded in existential–humanistic psychology and dialogical ethics, this emphasis explores the psychological roots of polarization and the internal landscapes that shape conflict. Students examine how fear, rigidity, and loss of perspective contribute to social divides and how presence, vulnerability, and deep listening can open pathways toward mutual recognition.

Drawing on models such as the Experiential Democracy Dialogue and Braver Angels' approaches to political depolarization, students engage with structured, relational techniques for initiating and sustaining transformative conversations. Emphasis is placed on the facilitator's inner work, recognizing that bridge building requires a cultivated capacity for humility, self-awareness, and emotional spaciousness. Through experiential practices, case study work, and community engagement, learners develop the tools needed to guide individuals and groups through difficult dialogues.

By the end of this course, students learn how to design and lead dialogue initiatives in communities, organizations, schools, and interdisciplinary contexts. The emphasis invites learners to embody the role of "citizen therapist"—a socially engaged healer who brings depth-oriented presence into civic spaces to foster connection, dignity, and shared humanity.

Learning Objectives

Students completing this emphasis will be able to:

1. Analyze psychological and existential dynamics underlying polarization and social fragmentation.
2. Facilitate structured and unstructured dialogues using depth-oriented, relational methods.
3. Apply dialogical ethics—presence, empathy, humility—in high-tension environments.
4. Identify and address internal barriers (biases, fears, defensiveness) that shape dialogue outcomes.
5. Integrate narrative, relational, and experiential tools to support healing across divides.
6. Evaluate dialogue frameworks and adapt them to diverse cultural and community contexts.
7. Design sustainable, community-based dialogue programs that support ongoing relational repair.
8. Embody grounded, ethical facilitation practices during conflict and relational rupture.
9. Support participants in exploring values, identity, and meaning as dimensions of civic healing.

Core Themes & Theoretical Foundations:

- Existential–humanistic/depth psychology
- Dialogical ethics
- Psychology of the polarized mind
- Narrative approaches to conflict
- Phenomenological presence and deep listening
- Democratic and civic engagement frameworks
- Community psychology

Depth-Oriented Psychotherapy for Underserved Communities

Course Description

This module prepares students to practice psychotherapy through a depth-oriented, culturally responsive, and justice-centered lens. Underserved communities—whether marginalized by race, gender, socioeconomic status, immigration status, disability, or systemic neglect—experience unique constellations of things like trauma, invisibility, and resilience. This course addresses the psychological, existential, and sociocultural impacts of oppression, while also honoring the inherent strengths and wisdom embedded in marginalized identities.

Drawing on humanistic, psychoanalytic, existential, and liberation psychologies, students explore how meaning-making, identity, cultural trauma, and relational wounds shape the therapeutic encounter. The emphasis challenges narrow definitions of "competence" and instead emphasizes relational humility, attunement, and an ongoing commitment to understanding power, privilege, and systemic contexts.

Students work with case material that includes experiences of microaggressions, cultural erasure, trauma of marginalization, and the existential pain of not being seen. Through experiential learning, dialogical inquiry, and community-grounded approaches, participants develop the capacity to offer psychotherapy that is both deeply personal and socially aware/affordable.

Learning Objectives

Students completing this emphasis will be able to:

1. Assess clinical presentations within the context of systemic inequities and cultural histories.
2. Apply humanistic, existential, and psychoanalytic tools in culturally responsive ways.
3. Recognize microaggressions, invisibility, and identity-based harm within therapy.
4. Establish therapeutic relationships grounded in dignity, presence, and cultural humility.
5. Integrate trauma-informed depth psychology into work with marginalized populations.

6. Explore existential themes—freedom, meaning, identity, alienation—in clients' lived experience.
7. Adapt therapeutic approaches to underserved settings with limited resources.
8. Critically examine power dynamics, transference, and countertransference through sociocultural lenses.
9. Design liberation-focused interventions that foster empowerment and resilience.

Core Themes & Theoretical Foundations

- Humanistic psychology and relational healing
- Liberation psychology
- Intersections of culture, trauma, and identity
- Psychoanalytic theories of cultural invisibility
- Existential therapy with marginalized populations
- The politics of presence
- Trauma of oppression and resilience

Applied Practice Settings

- Community mental health clinics
- Nonprofits serving BIPOC, LGBTQ+, immigrant, or houseless communities
- Correctional and reentry environments
- School-based mental health for marginalized youth
- Faith-based or community-based healing programs
- Crisis response and trauma recovery initiatives

Student Outcomes & Competencies

Graduates will gain skills in:

- Providing depth psychotherapy in low-resource or culturally complex environments
- Facilitating healing around identity, belonging, and systemic trauma
- Engaging in culturally grounded diagnostics and case formulation

- Practicing ethical, justice-oriented therapeutic presence
- Supporting existential meaning-making amidst adversity

Ideal Candidates/Who Should Enroll:
This emphasis is ideal for those called to serve communities historically excluded from high-quality mental health care. It is well suited for clinicians, advocates, healers, and community practitioners committed to relational justice, cultural responsiveness, and depth-informed practice.

As of this writing, the CODH Certificate Program has hosted two cohorts (in the spring/summer of 2025 and the fall/winter 2025) with approximately 80 students initially enrolled and 33 who have completed the course. Tyler and I have also been refining the course as we have learned more about both the difficulties—particularly technical and time allotment—and the attractions, chiefly concerning structure, articles and videos, and live interaction. We have also received a fascinating range of case studies illuminating how enrollees plan to apply their learning. Among the topics of these case studies are application of the bridge-building dialogues to a conflict between an immigrant and member of a host country as well as to a conflict regarding sexual identity between groups who hold secular identities and religious nationalists; longer term in-depth therapy was also proposed for students at a college counseling center who generally receive short-term symptom relief.

The emergence of interest in the CODH Certificate Program is attested to by comments by enrollees, such as the following [Names have been changed to protect confidentiality]:

> [Beth:] The more I observe it, the more I see how the system (including those corrupt billionaires) thrives on division, how it depends on us staying polarized and

distracted. And yet, what the world desperately needs right now is connection, empathy and depth.

That's why I've enrolled in the Corps of Depth Healers Certification....a twelve-week immersion in depth and existential psychology, which I know will be an incredible addition to my toolkit as a woman, mother and coaching practitioner.

As a mother and practitioner in the motherhood support space, I see my role not just as helping women flourish individually, but also helping to shift the systems and ideologies that keep so many of us (women AND men) stuck: outdated patriarchal values and policies, late-stage capitalism, inequitable workplaces, inflexible employers and the burnout it all breeds.

Real change—in ourselves, in our families, and in our culture—happens when we go deeper. When we slow down enough to listen, to question, and to reconnect with what matters.

[Cynthia]: My case study demonstrates how political polarization can challenge even professional communities dedicated to healing, revealing the emotional, identity-based, and relational dimensions of conflict that extend beyond policy disagreements. Applying the Braver Angels model and existential-humanistic principles highlights the importance of structured dialogue, facilitator self-awareness, and relational presence in bridging divides.

Integrating my personal bridge-building approach (grounded in curiosity, presence, and ethical commitment) reinforces the value of modeling openness and empathy in organizational interactions. These strategies directly inform concrete policies, ensuring that future conflicts are approached with intentional bridge-building practices rather than reactive measures.

Addressing polarization in professional counseling associations is more than procedural; it is an opportunity to model relational, ethical, and humanistic principles central to the profession. By institutionalizing these practices, associations can cultivate resilient, inclusive, and ethically grounded cultures capable of navigating both internal conflict and broader societal challenges.

[Liza:] I am finding the [course] concept very appealing and the materials very well designed. Am enjoying this course! I think that there is a gap between theory and practice that I look forward to bridging—the materials are powerful—especially about the gang work. I loved the exercise about "privilege," [the] social healing video, [the] Dao of Maslow, I and Thou really stick out as interesting. Less attracted to Paulo Frere "Pedagogy of Oppressed." I see how different strands of this work are linked—active listening, semi-structured dialogue—excellent.

[Dianne:] ...here we are, if we want DEPTH, how can I better protect my calendar to not "move toward efficiency and maximizing time" but create spaces for slow savoring? A somehow relevant example: I had to wait for my not-as-yet-driving teen. I had a bunch of fallow time in the car when I wished I could have been "spending" that time better elsewhere...and then I turned it around, and used it as a chance to read the "We Need Raw Awe" article. Something about the [mundaneness] of "killing time waiting" for my child while reading about "raw awe" was such a perfect contrast. There don't have to be perfect moments—we can find the awe even waiting in a freezing cold car! It was that coming together of the visceral experience coupled with the meaning I might lay and then overlay

> to create human experience that somehow seems like an important kernel; cultivating a sense of ALIVENESS in evermore moments I can manage and supporting others to do the same seems to me at the kernel of what I'm wanting to explore here.
>
> Regarding the content of what might be changed is that much of what's been offered in terms of readings has, I think, been written by White folks. In itself, that's fine. [But] I wonder what a course curriculum would be like to have it reflect the 80% of global majority folks. That said, I do appreciate the acknowledgment of systems of oppression, including racism. Really, I see this as the invitation for me to step into greater sharing my own perspectives, and, again, supporting others to do the same.
>
> This course is like a booster for depth, especially in a world that is increasingly transactional. It has instigated a renewed interest in meaning making and creativity that has enriched both my personal and professional life.

Finally, here's a lengthy yet poignant report from Joe, one of the graduates of the CODH Certificate Program who hosted a slightly modified Experiential Democracy Dialogue workshop in his living room. This report was created on February 23, 2026:

> Joe: Three days ago, 17 people sat in my living room for an experiment. A model called "Experiential Democracy Dialogue"—developed by a major figure in the American existential-humanistic psychology field, Prof. Kirk Schneider, aimed at helping people see and hear each other despite the differences.
>
> [The people in the group were] half religious, half secular. Carefully chosen—not from the extremes, but people willing to try something different. I chose

them carefully to enable this conversation. Even though I have been facilitating groups and workshops of my own for over 20 years, this was a new model for me. I had never experienced it before, just read about and got the outline. I liked it from the get-go: two people talk, I facilitate, six parts [or phases], very short, lots of mirroring. Slowing things down allows for better listening, less reactivity. They were here as themselves, not representing anyone else, not to debate, not to convince. To reflect, respond, listen, mirror, express.

The question we explored was simple—and not simple at all: When you think about the future of Israel as a Jewish and democratic state, what do you fear losing the most? And how should the state act to prevent that loss?

This question carries intellectual differences—but even more, it carries fear. Deep, visceral fear. These really are noisy, combative, fearful times.

For 45 minutes, we followed a structured dialogue model:

- No interruptions.
- No cross-talk.
- Short speaking times.
- Reflective listening.
- Then we opened the circle for a second round, keeping the same spirit.

What happened? No shouting. No attempts to convince. But real differences.

One participant said, "We didn't see that much difference."

Another said it felt "too sweet" — that maybe we're too used to conflict to trust this kind of listening.

There was one moment of anger—when a religious participant said that if forced to choose between "Jewish" and "democratic," he would choose "Jewish."

The reaction was strong. And yet—afterward, they spoke privately. They continued the conversation.

Several secular participants shared something that moved me deeply: they feel they lack knowledge of Jewish texts and regret that separation in our education system. Others spoke about fears for their children—religious and secular alike—that the appreciation of the other's humanity is being lost. A sharp 18-year-old shared how in a mixed youth movement he learned that once you truly know someone, most differences shrink.

One sentence stayed with me: "The biggest problem is that we don't know each other. We live in separate bubbles."

Was it perfect? No.

Was it enough to solve anything? Of course not. Obviously, the real difficult people were not in that room, they are out there toward the extremes, very likely that they would never come to such an event. And true—they are the ones who make the most noise.
But you need to start somewhere.

There is a place to "make lots of noise"—I certainly agree with that. But there are many places where that "noise" just does more damage than good. In the end we all need that human connection.

Something happened in that room.

For three hours, people practiced listening before reacting.

They practiced seeing the human being behind the position.

They created a small space where fear could soften into curiosity.

In a time when many feel exhausted, polarized, and wounded that feels meaningful.

I got lots of compliments, smiles, hugs and thanks. Those always feel good...

I don't know yet where this will lead.

> But I know this: Seeing the other is not naïve. It is disciplined work. And it gives me hope. To solve anything, create something, move somewhere and let creativity in, you have to first learn to listen, to really listen. This in itself is not easy.
>
> Feel proud to have done this and now...?

"And now?" indeed is the question for Joe and all his peers; the question of "where to go from here?" But given the recency of the Depth Healer certificate program and experiential dialogue format, this report is encouraging. In that light, I understand that Joe and several of his colleagues plan to continue developing the form of social healing they created through the certificate program.

Conclusion

I have no illusions about how difficult it is to forge a vibrant-centered society. This is a great and long-term task, especially in the face of statements like those by Stephen Miller. Miller, U.S. Homeland Security Advisor and close aide to the U.S. President, declared that: "We live in a world in which you can talk all you want about international niceties....But we live in a world, in the real world...[t]hat is governed by strength, that is governed by power. These are the iron laws of the world that have existed since the beginning of time"[1]

Miller has a point; we do live in a world that has long been dominated by (military) power. And in dire circumstances it becomes a necessity. But the use of power for self-defense, or as a last resort, is a very different thing than using it for the antiquated idea that "the spoils belong to the victors." It is a very different thing to use power to prevent a genocide or nuclear war than to deploy it to "take over" countries like Venezuela, which was the context for Miller's pronouncement, or to attack even smaller countries that pose little or no threat to the United States; to send federal troops to states like Minnesota, Oregon, and California in the absence of those states' requests; or to unleash a "wrecking ball" mentality to meet one person's (or party's) needs. There are grave concerns, for example, about the major operation underway during the writing of this book to subdue Iran.

Contrastingly, there are also limits to diversity politics and the reversal of justice to align chiefly with the oppressed. Despite eons of historical justification to align with these depleted groups, might we overidealize them at times as well? As social philosophers Albert Camus and Frantz Fanon warned (as we shall see), these groups can also become fanatical, culturally or religiously polarized, misogynist and imperialist—especially if their motivation sides more with vengeance than deliberation, fear rather than mindfulness (which admittedly is a very tall task for people who have been so dehumanized).[2] Yet the question still needs to be raised, even in these circumstances: What is the cost of *disenfranchized* versions of "cancel culture," or "my party right or wrong," or "us versus them," particularly for those who want to think and act more independently—more presently, openly, and discerningly? We've seen such predicaments among some of the great emancipators themselves, until they moved more toward a vibrant-centered, awe-based view. I'm thinking here of cultural icons like Malcolm X, who (understandably in some cases) equated Caucasians with "white devils" and called for a pan-African revolution "by any means necessary"— that is, until he traveled to Mecca to partake in the powerful Islamic pilgrimage called the Hajj.[3] There he not only interacted with people of many cultures and variations of skin color (including white), but he found a comradery among them that nudged him toward a renewed appreciation of humanity as a whole, regardless of ethnicity. I'm also thinking again of the great sociopolitical psychiatrist Frantz Fanon. He likewise held an understandable outrage toward the white world, and particularly white colonizers of the world. And he too justified the violent overthrow of those colonizers, similar to Malcom X, "by any means necessary." But Fanon also developed an appreciation for the complexity of that call and the need to temper it with a recognition of colonizers' humanity. He held the creative challenge of both ousting those oppressors while finding ways of acknowledging their dignity as human beings, of precisely avoiding the trap of repeating the dehumanization wrought upon themselves.[4]

What we see here is that neither fear-based imperialism nor vengeance-based rebellion tend to work out very well in the cycles of human history. They oppress, degrade, and destroy souls as much as lives, and they rarely achieve their often illusory objectives of conquest. What they do achieve, on the other hand, is bitterness, resentment, superficiality, and hate, a temporary high perhaps but an inevitable collapse. Camus brought this lack of present, deliberative, and discerning reactivity into the stark light of day in his powerful volume *The Rebel*. In this masterwork, he described "moderation" as a radical concept, more like the vibrant center and distinct from the moderation that ignores the need to rebel. He writes:

> Naturally, it is not a question of despising anything, or of exalting one civilization at the expense of another... Moderation is not the opposite of rebellion. Rebellion in itself is moderation, and it demands, defends, and recreates it throughout history and its eternal disturbances...Moderation, born of rebellion, can only live by rebellion. It is a perpetual conflict, continually created and mastered by the intelligence. It does not triumph either in the impossible or in the abyss. It finds its equilibrium through them.[5]

In sum, we're in deep trouble when we say in essence that "everything we're doing is right and everything they're doing is wrong." That's an "iron law" of history too—more iron, I contend, than Miller's statement implying "might is right."

We've got to dig deeper. We've got to actively engage with people of all stripes (short of being mortally threatened by them) if we are to make any advances in the mending of our broken worlds. This book is a testament to a dynamic middle ground—a ground of consciousness, choice, and responsiveness as distinct from drivenness routine, and reactivity. The onward thrust of technocracy will only intensify this distinction. We will need more consciousness, choice, and responsiveness, more presence, openness, and discernment—more awe for life—if we are to manage our devices versus their management of us. We will need enriching environments, enlivening caretakers, the encounter with life's paradoxes, the cultivation of authenticity, active worldliness, and abiding courage to creatively respond to the automation that is increasingly enveloping our lives.

In the short run, this crisis prods us to increase our live participation in social gatherings, pursue new religious and political leadership and expose ourselves to people, places, and things that challenge us. It prompts us to think, encourages us to seek more of what matters to us, and gives us ideas about how to live a more gratifying life. In the long run, the crisis presses us to integrate a vibrant-centered, awe-based consciousness in every major sector of our lives—from parenting and family relations to educational and work settings, and from religious and spiritual contexts to governmental and diplomatic arenas. Our task is formidable but, as attested to in this book, doable. The seeds and planters are here. Now we need to mobilize them and mobilize ourselves.

Appendix A

Keys to an Awe-Based, Vibrantly Centered Consciousness

- The time to reflect.
- Contemplative time alone.
- A focus on what one loves.
- In-depth therapy or meditation.
- A capacity to savor the moment.
- A capacity to see the big picture.
- An appreciation for the fact of life.
- An openness to the mystery of life and being.
- An appreciation of discovery and growth from engagement with others and that which is "other."
- An appreciation of pain as a sometime teacher.
- An ability to trust in the ultimately unknowable.
- Contemplative time with close friends or companions.
- Contemplative time in natural or non-distracting settings.
- An appreciation of balance (e.g., between one's fragility and resiliency).
- An ability to give oneself over, discerningly, to the ultimately unknowable.
- An ability to stay present to and accept the evolving nature of life and of conflict—for example, to know that "this too shall pass."

Appendix B (from Chapter 7)

There are many other studies that have supported the findings on resilient luminaries in addition to some of O'Connell Higgins and other researchers' findings. Consider Dean Keith Simonton's Key Criteria for Greatness:

- Prolific & Early Productivity: Great individuals produce a large volume of work early in life, often peaking in their late 30s/early 40s, showing deep commitment and talent from a young age (e.g., Mozart at 5, Bobby Fischer at 6).
- Novelty & Uniqueness: Their creations (ideas, artworks, theories) are original, possess a distinctive personal style, and are adaptable to their field's problems, leaving an indelible mark.
- High Social Impact: Their work profoundly affects others, changing how people think, behave, or experience the world, evident in citations, historical consensus, or societal shifts.
- Openness to Experience: They possess broad interests (travel, languages, arts) beyond their core domain, which fuels creativity.
- Persistence and Hard Work: Greatness involves immense effort and overcoming numerous failures, even if these failures aren't publicly highlighted.
- Intellectual Power: A crucial ingredient is deep intellectual capacity, leading to insightful, significant, and complex work.
- Bibliometric measures: This criterion utilized number of publications, art works, citations, and cross-validations across populations.

- Maslow's criteria for self-actualizing individuals: accurate reality perception, acceptance, spontaneity, problem-centering (focus on purpose), autonomy, deep relationships, creativity, and a sense of humor; valuing truth, beauty, goodness, and wholeness (B-values), noting they reach this peak by fulfilling lower needs and pursuing their unique potential; ability to not only tolerate but thrive on contrasts, contradictions, and anxieties of living. Examples: exhibiting qualities such as childlikeness but also extraordinary maturity, individuality but also social consciousness, firmness but also tenderness.

Endnotes

Preface

[1]R. May, *Man's Search for Himself* (Norton, 1953): 69.

[2]See K. Schneider, *The Polarized Mind: Why It's Killing Us and What We Can Do About It* (University Professors Press, 2013) and K. Schneider & M. Fatemi, "Today's Biggest Threat: The Polarized Mind," *Scientific American*, April 16, 2019.

[3]E. Doherty, "New Poll Shows What Americans Think of America, and It's Not Great," *Politico,* November 2, 2025. https://www.politico.com/news/2025/11/02/poll-american-dream-polarization-00632538 and J. Haidt, *The Anxious Generation: How the Great Rewiring of Childhood is Causing an Epidemic of Mental Illness* (Penguin, 2024).

A Note About Method

[1]For an elaboration on my personal experience of the vibrant center (or what I once called the "fluid center") see K. Schneider, *Life-enhancing Anxiety: Key to a Sane World* (University Professors Press, 2023) and K. Schneider, in J. Falk & L. Hoffman (Eds.) *Becoming an Existential Humanistic Therapist: Narratives from the Journey* (University Professors Press, 2022): Chapter 2.

[2]E. Becker, *The Denial of Death* (Free Press, 1973): 285.

Introduction

[1]Presence, which can be defined colloquially as "really being there with one's whole-body awareness," or more formally as "the holding and illuminating of that which is palpably significant within a person and between a person and others," is the basis for openness and discernment (or deeply considered judgment). Indeed, presence appears foundational for psychological health. Put in the language of therapy outcome researchers, presence and its corollaries—openness and discernment—appear to be necessary conditions for the "relational and contextual factors"

researchers identify as most critical for effective psychotherapy. Among these factors are the therapeutic alliance, empathy, warmth, genuineness, the willingness to collaborate and work through ruptures, and the ongoing openness to change. For an elaboration of the above see C. Bradshaw, *The Client Experience of Therapeutic Presence* (Saybrook University, doctoral dissertation, 2024); S. Geller & L. Greenberg, *Therapeutic Presence: A Mindful Approach to Effective Therapeutic Relationships* (American Psychological Association, 2nd ed., 2023); K. Schneider, "Presence: The Core Contextual Factor of Effective Psychotherapy," Existential Analysis, 26.2: 304–312.

[2]I distinguish the "vibrant center" from Arthur Schlessinger's 1949 conception of the "vital center" (see A. Schlessinger, *The Vital Center: Politics of* Freedom, Routledge, 1997/1949). Whereas the vibrant center applies to the dynamism of an entire life-philosophy, from child-rearing to education and from work and religious affiliation to governance, the vital center refers chiefly to a centrist political position—one that weaves a path between capitalism and communism.

[3]See K. Schneider, *The Polarized Mind* (University Professors Press, 2013).

[4]See R. Sternberg's "balance theory of wisdom" in R. Sternberg & J. Gluck, *Wisdom* (Cambridge University Press, 2022).

Chapter 1: The Vibrant Center of Parenting

[1] The seeds for this primal sense of "groundlessness and helplessness" are powerfully introduced in O. Rank's *The Trauma of Birth* (Dover, 1993/1924) and Ernest Becker's *The Denial of* Death, and pursued later in Irvin Yalom's *Existential Psychotherapy* (Basic Books, 1980), Robert Kramer's *Otto Rank and the Creation of Modern Psychotherapy* (Oxford University Press, 2025) and my own volumes *Existential-Humanistic Therapy* (with Orah Krug, 2026, APA Publishing) and *Life-Enhancing Anxiety.*

[2]The significance of being "met" is superbly articulated by D.W. Winnicott (see D. Winnicott, *The Maturational Processes and the Facilitating Environment* [International Universities Press, 1965]).

[3]See C. McHugh's "Elon Musk's 'Move Fast and Break Things' Attitude Clashes with Washington," *Politico,* December, 24, 2024. (Accessed 3/6/26: https://www.politico.com/news/magazine/2024/12/24/elon-musk-washington-congress-00196006).

[4]See S. James, "Trumps DOJ Lashes Out at 'Dope' Reporter Over Epstein Files Complaint," *Yahoo! News*, December, 24, 2026. (Accessed 3/6/26: https://www.yahoo.com/news/articles/trump-doj-lashes-dope-reporter-161051595.html and L. Kellman's "Trump Ventures Deeper Into Anti-Immigrant Language By Calling People from Somalia 'Garbage, '*Associated Press*, 12/5/25. (Accessed 3/6/26, https://apnews.com/article/trump-garbage-somalia-minneapolis-immigrant-omar-03e31bba53519d8a39b419679a3b75d9e).

[5]W. Yeats, "The Second Coming," In C. Bain, J. Beaty, & J. Hunter, *Norton Anthology of Literature* (Norton, 1977): 844.

[6]Although there are some limitations in Baumrind's research, her basic typology of permissive, authoritative, authoritarian, and latest category, neglectful/uninvolved parenting, has generally held up well in the literature. See S. Cuppens & E. Ceulemans, "A Closer Look at a Well-Known Concept," *Journal of Child and Family Studies*, Sep 18, 2019, 28.1:168–181. doi: 10.1007/s10826-018-1242-x

[7] For an elaboration on the need for a dynamic balance between healthy boundaries and risk-taking, the need for parental guidance but also personal empowerment and development of self-responsibility, especially in boys, see S. Galloway, *Notes on Being a Man* (Simon & Schuster, 2025).

[8]See K. Schneider, *Awakening to Awe: Personal Stories of Profound Transformation* (Jason Aronson, 2009).

[9]See W. Whitman, *Song of Myself*, (Poetry Foundation, 1892): Section 51. (Accessed 3/10/26: https://www.poetryfoundation.org/poems/45477/song-of-myself-1892-version).

For a succinct summary of the Buddhist view of impermanence, see H. Smith, *The Religions of Man* (Harper & Row, 1986); and for a synopsis of deconstructionism, see S. Glendinning, *Derrida: A Very Short Introduction* (Oxford University Press, 2011).

[10]B. Pascal, "Penses," in M. Friedman's *The Worlds of Existentialism: A Critical Reader* (Humanities Press, 1991/1654): 41; O. Rank, *The Psychology of the Soul: A Study of the Origin, Conceptual Evolution, and Nature of the Soul* (Johns Hopkins University Press, 1998/1930).

[11]A. Heschel, *Man is Not Alone: A Philosophy of Religion* (Farrar, Straus, & Giroux, 1951): 26.

[12]In keeping with the existential–humanistic tradition (e.g., see Tillich's concept of "listening love" in this volume), I view what might be called "resonance validity" or the whole-body

deliberation over a given personal or ethical decision as the best we can do in forming decisions that deeply matter to us. They are not absolute in any foundational sense and subject to change in the light of new evidence. But they do seem to be both more humane and substantive than decisions made in the absence of such centering. See also L. Hoffman, S. Stewart, & L. Meek, "Toward a Sustainable Myth of Self: An Existential Response to the Postmodern Condition," *Journal of Humanistic Psychology,* 2009, 49.2. doi.org/10.1177/0022167808324880.

[13]M. Angelou, "That Which Lives After Us," in P. Woodruff & H. Wilmer, *Facing Evil: Light at the Core of Darkness* (Open Court, 1988): 22.

[14]May, *Man's search for himself*: 146.

[15]Heschel, *Man is Not Alone*: 77.

Chapter 2: The Vibrant Center of Education

[1]See K. Schneider, *The Depolarizing of America: A Guide to Social Healing* (University Professors Press, 2020) and Schneider, *Life-Enhancing Anxiety* for an elaboration. The Experiential Democracy Dialogue draws from many existential and depth psychological sources, but Martin Buber's "I–Thou" relationship is central to this lineage. See M. Buber, *I and Thou* (Charles Scribners' Sons, 1970). There are also contemporary influencers who endorse greater "I–Thou" style dialogue in our society, such as feminist theorist Judith Butler; see "Judith Butler at the University of Manchester," 2025. https://www.youtube.com/watch?v=njSljXwTn0g&t=431s and talk show host Bill Maher, *Real Time* with Bill Maher, HBO cable television.

[2]See H. Levitt & Z. Morrill, "Power Issues in Psychotherapy and How Contemporary Humanistic–Existential Approaches Address Them," in L. Hoffman, L. Vallejos, D. Hocoy, P. Tummala-Nara, & E. DeRobertis (Eds.), *APA Handbook of Humanistic and Existential Psychology,* Vol. 2: 335–349; and Z. Morrill & L. Comas-Díaz, "Critical-liberation Psychotherapy: Unsettling Hegemonic Power Toward Liberatory Practice," *American Psychologist,* Vol. 80(4): 576–588. doi.org/10.1037/amp0001444.

[3]See W. Anderson, *The Upstart Spring: Esalen and the American Awakening* (Addison-Wesley, 1983).

[4]E. Gaugele & M. Schieren, "Reprocessing the Body of Racial Trauma: Multidirectional Memory and Decolonizing Somatic Workshops in Art/ Performance," *Parse,* 2002,*15*(Autumn). https://parsejournal.com/article/re-processing-the-body-of-racial-

trauma/#:~:text=First%2C%20the%20labor%20on%20"interpersonal,of%20human%20and%20social%20change

[5]This summary is adapted from *The Depolarizing of America.* The book's credo, which echoes that of the conflict mediation organization Braver Angels, is curiosity, respect, and openness, enhancing the prospect of achieving common ground. It is highly recommended that dialogue partners review the aforementioned book, as well as the Corps of Depth Healers' YouTube channel, to attain the optimal background for this dialogue process. Generally, this dialogue process is most effective when facilitated by a skilled and knowledgeable mediator and when dialogue partners have the desire and ability to adhere to the format's ground rules.

[6]Although I didn't directly intend this, "openness" and "discernment" are closely associated with two traits from the so-called Big Five Personality Factors, "openness" and "conscientiousness." Both consistently correlated with well-being and negatively correlated with neuroticism. See W. Kang, F. Stephens, S. Pineda, K. Widich, & A. Malvaso, "Personality Traits and Dimensions of Mental Health," *Scientific Reports,* 2023. https://www.nature.com/articles/s41598-023-33996-1

[7] The Heterodox Academy is a grass-roots organization that promotes cultures of open inquiry in academia. Their website is heterodoxacademy.org. See also Haidt, *The Anxious Generation* (Penguin, 2024) and D. Goleman, *Emotional Intelligence: Why it Can Matter More than IQ* (Bantam, 2005).

[8]See R. May, *The Cry for Myth* (Norton, 1991).

[9]B. Devereaux, "Colleges Should be More than Just Vocational Schools," *New York Times,* April 2, 2023.

Chapter 3: The Vibrant Center of Work

[1]W. Smith & M. Lewis, *Both/And Thinking: Embracing the Creative Tensions to Solve Your Toughest Problems* (Harvard Business Review Press, 2022) 94.

[2]See the interview with life-coach Yannick Jacobs on "The Art of Existential Coaching: Yannick Jacob on Meaning, Purpose, and Resilience," podcast *Depth Dialogues.* Accessed March 14, 2026: https://www.youtube.com/watch?v=y3oSOZUKvxU

[3]This survey is from a study sponsored by the American Psychological Association titled "Majority of U.S. Workers Say Job Insecurity Has

Significant Impact on Their Stress: Highlights from the 2025 Work in America™ Survey. (Accessed August 5, 2025, https://www.apa.org/pubs/reports/work-in-america/2025).

Chapter 4: The Vibrant Center of Religion and Spirituality

[1]D. Berger, Director; P. Straughan, Screenwriter, *Conclave* (Distributed by Black Bear, U.K., and Focus Features, U.S., 2024).

[2]F. Scott Fitzgerald, *The Great Gatsby* (Charles Scribner's Sons, 1925/1953).

[3]See P. Tillich, *The Dynamics of Faith* (Harper-Torchbooks, 1957).

[4]Berger & Straughan, *Conclave.*

[5] Berger & Straughan, *Conclave.*

[6]Schneider, *Life-Enhancing Anxiety.*

[7]Cited in J. Needleman, *What is God?* (Tarcher/Penguin, 2009): 148.

[8]"Listening love" is discussed in P. Tillich, *My Search for Absolutes* (Simon & Schuster, 1967): 109-111; and the "I-Thou" relationship is elucidated in M. Buber, *I and Thou.*

[9]Schneider, *The Polarized Mind.*

[10]P. Tillich, "The Lost Dimension in Religion" (*Saturday Evening Post,* June 14, 1958). See also M. Fox, *Creation Spirituality: Liberating Gifts for the People of the Earth* (Harper-San Francisco, 1991) and O. Rank, *Beyond Psychology* (published by friends and students of the Author, 1941).

[11] These are the kinds of questions now being asked with greater intensity by politicians like Texas Senatorial candidate James Talarico. See E. Klein, "James Talarico's Beautiful Answer to Christian Nationalism," January 13, 2026. (Accessed 3/15/26, https://www.youtube.com/watch?v=sa6fiO2EgJ4).

[12] These findings derive from "moral foundations theory." See C. Erentzen, T. Wei-Ting Chao, & A. Chasteen, "Caring to a Fault: Perceived Moral Difference Between the Self and Muslim "Others" as a Predictor of Islamophobia," *Psychology of Religion and Spirituality,* 2025, *17*: 115.

[13]See A. Gopnik, "Why Are Americans Still Uncomfortable With Atheism?" *New Yorker,* October 29, 2018: 72–76.

[14]See Schneider, *Life-Enhancing Anxiety*, Chapter 16 as well as the passages on "mystical agnosticism," in K. Armstrong, *A History of God* (Ballantine Books, 1993) and "radical amazement" in Heschel, *Man is Not Alone*:13.

Chapter 5: The Vibrant Center of Government

1By "psychospiritual" I mean an approach that is inclusive of the fuller ranges of human experiences, from the physiological and behavioral and the cognitive and psychodynamic to the experiential and transcendent. A simpler way to put this is that the psychospiritual refers to what Tillich calls the "depth dimension" (see Note 39) or the "whole body" experience of living to the degree one can engage that. I believe that our psychological leaders should have a working familiarity with each of those ranges of experience. See also J. Needleman, *The American Soul: Rediscovering the Wisdom of the Founders* (Tarcher, 2003) for a wonderful elaboration on how psychospirituality can and has played a critical role in American governance.

2"Multeity in Unity" was introduced in S. Coleridge, "On the Principles of Genial Criticism of the Fine Arts," *Felix Farley's Bristol Journal,* August–September, 1814. See also R. Bellah, R. Madsen, W. Sullivan, A. Swidler, & S. Tipton, *Habits of the Heart: Individualism and Commitment in American Life* (University of California Press, 1996). The latter is a communitarian attempt to embody "multeity in unity" and support a vibrant centered politics.

3 See T. Snyder, *On Tyranny: 20 Lessons from the Twentieth Century* (Penguin Random House, 2017) for an elaboration on both the Marshall Plan and Nazi Germany's collapse.

4M. Buber, *At the Turning: Three Addresses on Judaism* (New York: Farrar, Straus, and Young, 1952).

5For an elaboration on the basis for an Office of Psychological Advisors, see K. Schneider, "The U.S. Needs a Mental Health Czar," *Scientific American* 2019, November: 12, and "Why Biden Needs to Appoint a Psychological Advisor," *Smerconish.com*, October 27, 2021. https://www.smerconish.com/exclusive-content/why-biden-needs-to-appoint-a-psychological-advisor/

6 See J. Haidt, *The Anxious Generation* and Snyder, *Tyranny* for elaborations on the above points.

7 This research is exemplified by such groups as "More in Common." See "New Report from More in Common Reveals that Most Americans Are Interested in Connecting Across Differences—But Lack the Opportunities To Do So," More in Common, March 18, 2025. https://moreincommonus.com/press_release/new-report-from-more-in-common-reveals-that-most-americans-are-interested-in-connecting-across-difference-but-lack-opportunities-to-do-so/ See also H. Baron, R. Blair, D. Choi, L.

Gamboa, J. Gottlieb, A. Robinson, S. Rosenzweig, M. Turnbull, & E. West, "Couples Therapy for a Divided America: Assessing the Effects of Reciprocal Group Reflection on Partisan Polarization," *Political Behavior,* October 16, 2024.

[8] E. Mudryk, A. Lee, C. Geraci, & L. Johnson, "For You Are With Me: The Relationship Between Religious Coping Styles and Mental Health Symptoms Among Black Americans," *Practice Innovations* 2025, *10*: 292.

[9]T. Jackson, Personal Communication, February 27, 2020. See also Community Healing Network, "Emotional Emancipation Circles." https://communityhealingnet.org/engage/#Rapid-Response-Ubuntu-Healing-Circles

[10]R. Magee, *The Inner Work of Social Justice*: *Healing Ourselves and Transforming Our Communities Through Mindfulness* (Tarcher-Perigee, 2019).

[11]See also M. O'Reilly Landry, "To Heal from Covid America Must Fix Its Psychological Infrastructure," *Smerconish.com*, September 8, 2021. https://www.smerconish.com/exclusive-content/to-heal-from-covid-america-must-fix-its-psychological-infrastructure/

[12]The quotes in this segment are from Braver Angels, "Braver Politics to Bridge the Partisan Divide," December 19, 2024.

Chapter 6: Are We Ready for a Political Party Called 'The Vibrant Center?"

[1] L. Sanders & A. Thomson-Deveaux, "Young Americans Are Increasingly Rejecting the Democratic and Republican Parties New Poll Shows," *San Francisco Chronicle,* January 12, 2026. https://www.sfchronicle.com/news/politics/article/more-americans-identify-as-political-21290472.php

[2]See A. Maslow, *The Farther Reaches of Human Nature* (Penguin, 1971) on "D" (or deficiency motivation) vs. "B" (or Being motivation) as a part of his hierarchy of needs paradigm.

[3]See R. Reich, *Coming Up Short: A Memoir of My America* (Knopf, 2025); and J. Stigletz, *The Great Divide: Unequal Societies and What We Can Do About Them* (Norton, 2016).

[4]O. Ullman, *Empathy Economics: Janet Yellen's Remarkable Rise to Power and Her Drive to Spread Prosperity to All* (Public Affairs, 2022).

[5] See T. Pauchant and Associates, *In Search of Meaning: Managing for the Health of Our Organizations, Our Communities, and the Natural World* (Jossey-Bass, 1995) and W. Smith & M. Lewis, *Both/and*

Thinking: Embracing Creative Tensions To Solve Your Toughest Problems (Harvard Business Review Press, 2022) .

[6]This is also the essential message of classic works like Simone de Beauvoir's *The Ethics of Ambiguity* (Citadel, 1962). In this slim volume, she argues that deep reflection and struggle are virtual prerequisites for substantive ethical stances.

[7]See H. Arendt, *The Origins of Totalitarianism* (Harcourt, Brace Jovanovich, 1973) and Snyder, *On Tyranny.*

[8]On this latter point, see B. Schneider, *The Unfinished Metropolis: Igniting the City-Building Revolution* (Island Press, 2025).

[9] D. Brooks, "America Needs a Mass Movement—Now!," *The Atlantic,* November 2025. https://www.theatlantic.com/magazine/archive/2025/11/autocracy-resistance-social-movement/684336/?utm_source=newsletter&utm_medium=email&utm_campaign=the-atlantic-am&utm_term=The%20Atlantic%20AM

Chapter 7: Toward an Awe-Based, Vibrantly Centered World

[1]G. O'Connell Higgins, *Resilient Adults: Overcoming a Cruel Past* (Jossey-Bass, 1994): xiii.

[2]O'Connell Higgins, *Resilient Adults*: xiii–xiv.

[3]The concept of a "helpful" or "sympathetic" witness is elaborated in A. Miller, *The Untouched Key: Tracing Childhood Trauma in Creativity and Destructiveness* (Knopf-Doubleday, 1991).

[4]O'Connell Higgins, *Resilient Adults*: 68–71, 114.

[5]R. Graber, R. Turner., & A. Madill, "Best Friends and Better Coping: Facilitating Psychological Resilience through Boys' and Girls' Closest Friendships, *British Journal of Psychology*, 2016, 107(2): 338–358. doi.org/10.1111/bjop.12135

[6]O'Connell Higgins, *Resilient Adults,* 114.

[7]O'Connell Higgins, *Resilient Adults,* 115.

[8]O'Connell Higgins, *Resilient Adults,* 115.

[9] O'Connell Higgins, *Resilient Adults,* 117.

[10]O'Connell Higgins, *Resilient Adults,* 174–175.

[11]K. Schneider, *Rediscovery of Awe: Splendor, Mystery, and the Fluid Center of Life* (Paragon House, 2004).

[12]S. Batchelor, *Buddhism Without Beliefs: A Contemporary Guide to Awakening* (Riverhead Books, 1998); P. Tillich, *Dynamics of Faith*: K. Schneider, *Awakening to Awe.*

[13]O'Connell Higgins, *Resilient Adults,* 228.

[14]O'Connell Higgins, *Resilient Adults,* 229.

[15] A. Masten, *Ordinary Magic: Resilience in Development* (Guilford, 2014): 148.

[16]G. Bonnano, *The End of Trauma: How the New Science of Resilience is Changing How We Think About PTSD* (Basic Books, 2024).

[17]For a similar finding about the cross-cultural nature of self-actualizing individuals, see S. Kaufman, *Transcend: The New Science of Self-Actualization* (Penguin-Random House, 2020): 90.

[18]See V. Frankl, *Recollections: An Autobiography* (Basic Books, 1997) and A. Pattakos, *Prisoners of Our Thoughts: Viktor Frankl's Principles at Work* (Gildan Audio and Blackstone Publishing, 2021).

[19]See Frankl, *Recollections.*

[20]See Frankl, *Recollections.*

[21]See Frankl, *Recollections* on Frankl's social democratic activism; R. May, *Existential Psychology* (Random House, 1961): 42, on strains of authoritarianism in Frankl's practice; L. Langer, "The Lie of Viktor Frankl," Tablet Magazine, 2018 on Frankl's alleged performance of lobotomies. In fairness, however, Frankl's therapeutic approach has been embraced by many other therapists and patients, and has been updated in more personable and client-centered forms exemplified by the work of Alfried Langle, who was a protégé of Frankl (e.g., see S. Langle & C. Wurm, *Living Your Own Life: Existential Analysis in Action* (Rouledge, 2016). Also, Frankl's psychosurgeries, including highly selective lobotomies, appear to have been performed in accordance with the standards of his times and for very desperate patients.

[22]Much of this biographical background was drawn from https://en.wikipedia.org/wiki/Nelson_Mandela; the quote from Mandela is from J. Sithole, "Nelson Mandela: The Making of a Troublemaker," March 18, 2023. https://web.stanford.edu/class/e297a/Nelson%20Mandella.htm

[23] The above quotes are from Sithole, "Nelson Mandela."

[24]City Year Columbus Americorps Member, "Imagine a World Where Ubuntu is the Norm," November, 14, 2019. https://www.cityyear.org/columbus/stories/the-corps/imagining-a-world-where-ubuntu-is-the-norm/

[25] N. Mandela, "Renewal and Renaissance: Toward a New World Order," Lecture delivered at Oxford Center for Islamic Studies, Oxford, England, July 11, 1997.

[26]See S. Segal, *Mandela's Leadership Legacy* (Routledge, 2026) for a wonderful philosophical and psychological reflection on Mandela's life and influence.

[27]This television program is transcribed in Angelou, "That Which Lives After Us."

[28]Angelou, "That Which Lives After Us," 22.

[29] Discussion of Uncle Willie: Angelou, "That Which Lives After Us," 25.

[30]Angelou, "That Which Lives After Us," 26.

[31] Angelou, "That Which Lives After Us," 27.

[32] Angelou, "That Which Lives After Us," 27.

[33] Angelou, "That Which Lives After Us," 29.

[34]L. Denfield quoted in Sherriff J. Knight & Staff, "Remembering Dr. Maya Angelou: 1928–2014." https://mayaangelou.wfu.edu/maya-angelou-guestbook/comment-page-12/#:~:text=thoughts%20are%20things".-,Dr.,Obviously%20Dr.

[35]The quote immediately above is from Guy Johnson, KRON 4 Television, *Poet Maya Angelou's Son, Guy Johnson Passes Away,* 2022. https://www.youtube.com/watch?v=bdB9yYUMSlc

[36]See "Stephen Hawking Biography." https://www.notablebiographies.com /Gi-He/Hawking-Stephen.html as well as https://en.wikipedia.org/wiki/Stephen_Hawking#:~:text=Stephen%20William%20Hawking%20(8%20January,at%20the%20University%20of%20Cambridge

[37]S. Hawking, *My Brief History* (Penguin Random House, 2018).

[38] L. Gregory, "A Message from Stephen Hawking: It Can Be Done," Delivered at the *World Economic Forum's Annual Meeting* as part of the session on "Sustainable Development: A Message for the Future." The United Nations Sustainable Development Summit took place in New York on September 25–27, 2015. https://medium.com/@elilgreN0W/a-message-from-stephen-hawking-it-can-be-done-1200bce0d744

[39]Drawn from biographical information about Thich Nhat Hanh and his Plum Village. https://plumvillage.org/about/thich-nhat-hanh/ biography and https://en.wikipedia.org/wiki/Thích_Nhất_Hạnh

[40]D. Simmonton, *Greatness: Who Makes History and Why* (Guilford Press, 1994).

[41]Cited in E. Herklotz, "History in the Making: Thich Nhat Hanh," *16*: 394. https://scholarworks.lib.csusb.edu/cgi/viewcontent.cgi?article=1295&context=history-in-the-making

[42]Cited in Herklotz, "History in the Making," 395.

[43]Cited in Herklotz, "History in the Making," 395.

[44]Quotes from M. Haight, "75 Quotes from Thich Nhat Hanh to Inspire You to Live a Better Life," *Audibleblog,* September 18, 2025. https://www.audible.com/blog/quotes-thich-nhat-hanh

[45]Paraphrased from E. Haseley, "Simone de Beauvoir (1908–1986)." *Towards Emancipation? Women in European History.* https://hist259.web.unc.edu/simonedebeauvoir-2/#:~:text=Born%20in%20January%201908%20in,of%20the%20unnaturalness%20of%20marriage

[46] S. de Beauvoir, *The Second Sex* (Vintage, 2007/1949).

[47]See S. Cleary, "For Beauvoir, It's Friendship That Let's Us Be Truly Ourselves," *Psyche,* October 11, 2022. https://psyche.co/ideas/for-beauvoir-its-friendship-that-lets-us-become-truly-ourselves and E. Haseley, "Simone de Beauvoir (1908–1986)."

[48]de Beauvoir, *Ethics of Ambiguity.*

[49]de Beauvoir, *Ethics of Ambiguity.* 133, 153, 67, 106, 134 (pages on which each of the key themes appear in the order of presentation).

[50]X. Wang, "Spiritual Warrior in Search of Meaning: An Existential View of Lu Xun Through His Life Incidents and Analogies," In L. Hoffman, M. Yang, F. Klaklauskas, A. Chan, & M. Mansilla (Eds.), *Existential Psychology East-West,* Vol. 1: 167. See also W. Xiaoming, "Lu Xun: Chinese Writer," *Encyclopedia Britannica* online. https://www.britannica.com/biography/Lu-Xun

[51]Wang, "Spiritual Warrior in Search of Meaning," 168.

[52]Wang, "Spiritual Warrior in Search of Meaning," 167.

[53]From "On the positive side" to "What is the root cause of the problem?" all quotes are from Wang, "Spiritual Warrior in Search of Meaning, 168.

[54]Wang, "Spiritual Warrior in Search of Meaning," 170.

[55]See Wang, "Spiritual Warrior in Search of Meaning."

[56]Wang, "Spiritual Warrior in Search of Meaning," 170–171.

[57]M. Zhu, "Lu Xun's Love and His Family," Sina.com.cn, February 25, 2004. http://edu.sina.com.cn/en/2004-02-25/19063.html#:~:text=Zhu %20is%20before%20her%20own,she%20had%20been%20seriously%20sick

[58]Wang, "Spiritual Warrior in Search of Meaning," 180.

[59]For an elaboration on Said's childhood, see https://en.wikipedia.org/wiki/Edward_Said#:~:text=Said's%20childhood%20was%20split%20between,as%20far%20away%20as%20possible.%22

[60]https://en.wikipedia.org/wiki/Edward_Said#:~:text=Said's%20childhood%20was%20split%20between,as%20far%20away%20as%20possible.%22.

[61] C. Hibri, "Edward Said's Groundbreaking Book Explained." *The Conversation,* February 12, 2023. https://theconversation.com/orientalism-edward-saids-groundbreaking-book-explained-197429#:~:text=Said%20analyses%20a%20vast%2C%20organised,justifies%20Western%20colonialism

[62]Hibri, "Edward Said's Groundbreaking Book Explained."

[63]"Orientalism by Edward Said, Afterward, and Preface," *Books and Boots: Reflections on Books and Art,* 2023. https://astrofella.wordpress.com/ 2023/09/25/orientalism-edward-said-afterword-preface/#:~:text= But%20then%2C%20in%20an%20effort,that%20it's%20an%20empirical%20fact

[64] E. Said, *Orientalism* (updated edition, Penguin, 2003): xxii.

[65]https://en.wikipedia.org/wiki/Edward_Said#:~:text=Said's%20childhood%20was%20split%20between,as%20far%20away%20as%20possible.%22

[66]R. Khalek, "Growing Up as Edward Said's Daughter: Najla Said on Palestinian Identity and Activism at Columbia," *Dispatches,* March 31, 2025. https://www.youtube.com/watch?v=pWUllmtv1R8

[67]For an elaboration see https://en.wikipedia.org/wiki/Edward_Said#:~:text=Said's%20childhood%20was%20split%20between,as%20far%20away%20as%20possible.%22 and M. Howe, "For Edward Said, Schultz Session Proved Cordial and Constructive," *New York Times,* March 28, 1988: https://www.nytimes.com/1988/03/28/world/for-edward-said-shultz-session-proved-collegial-and-constructive.html#:~:text=Occasionally%20the%20digitization%20process%20introduces,routine%20consultation%20with%20prominent%20Palestinians

[68]Quoted in J. Gili, *Lorca* (Penguin, 1960), xii. See also Universo Lorca on the influence of Lorca's father. https://shorturl.at/S6t8K and LA Opera Blog, "Federico Garcia Lorca: A Life of Art, Passion and Tragedy," August 3, 2025. https://www.laopera.org/discover-la-opera/explore/
blog/federico-garcia-lorca-a-life-of-art,-passion,-and-tragedy
as well as "Federico Garcia Lorca" for elaboration of Lorca's childhood, education, and artistic community. https://en.wikipedia.org/wiki/Federico_García_Lorca)

[69]Quoted in Gili, *Lorca,* xii.

[70] See Gili, *Lorca,* xiii-xxiii on these ancient and modern sensibilities.

[71] See Gili, *Lorca,* 127-139 on Lorca's vital concept of "duende."

[72]See R. May, *Courage to Create* (Norton, 1975).

[73]Quoted in Gili, *Lorca,* 128 and 132.
[74]See Gili, *Lorca*, xiv.
[75]See "Federico Garcia Lorca" (accessed via https://en.wikipedia.org/wiki/Federico_García_Lorca).
[76]Staff, Multnomah County Library, "Andrei Tarkovsky: Films and Resources." (Accessed March 24, 2026, https://multcolib.bibliocommons.com/v2/
list/display/87527376/100929432).
[77]N. Tataro, "Andrey Tarkovsky: A Cinema of Prayer," *Offscreen*, 2023. https://offscreen.com/view/andrey-tarkovsky-a-cinema-of-prayer-andrey-a-tarkovsky-2019#:~:text=That%20Tarkovsky's%20religious/spiritual%20undertaking,and%20physically%20farther%20from%20Russia
[78]Solaris Quotes, *IMBD*. (Accessed March 24, 2026, https://www.imdb.com/title/tt0069293/
quotes/?item=qt3095446).
[79]For an elaboration on these biographical points see N. Kornatsky, "10 Facts about Film Director Andrei Tarkovsky that You Should Know," *Gateway to Russia,* April 4, 2022. https://www.gw2ru.com/arts/3746-andrei-tarkovsky-facts and "Andrei Tarkovsky." (Accessed March 24, 2026, https://en.wikipedia.org/wiki/Andrei_Tarkovsky#:~:text=Andrei%20Tarkovsky%20was%20born%20in,conceal%20during%20the%20Soviet%20days).
[80]A. Tarkovski, *Sculpting in Time* (University of Texas, 1986): 36–37.
[81]Tarkovski, *Sculpting in Time,* 233, 236.
[82]Sadly, I need to acknowledge the tarnished personal life of Caesar Chavez, which has recently come to light. This example shows how vibrantly centered consciousness in one major area does not necessarily translate to other realms, although generally speaking, I contend that most of the resilient people I have highlighted in this volume show a greater congruence between their personal and professional lives. See M. Fernandez & S. Hurtes, "Caesar Chavez, A Civil Rights Icon, is Accused of Abusing Girls for Years," *New York Times*, March 18, 2026. https://www.nytimes.com/2026/03/18/us/cesar-chavez-sexual-abuse-allegations-ufw.html
[83]The full Depth Healer Certificate Program, including details on how to enroll as well as course description can be accessed via https://www.corpsofdepthhealers.com
[84]See https://www.corpsofdepthhealers.com/certificate-program as well as K. Schneider & T. Gamlen, "Bridging the Gap: Depth

Psychology and Social Healing," *Society for Humanistic Psychology Newsletter,* November, 2023. https://www.apadivisions.org/division-32/publications/newsletters/humanistic/2023/11/depth-psychology-social-healing

[85]This detailed overview of the CODH Certificate Program curriculum is available only to enrollees via https://www.corpsofdepthhealers.com/certificate-program.

Conclusion

[1]Quoted by K. Rogers, "Stephen Miller Offers a Strongman View of the World," *New York Times,* January 6, 2026. https://www.nytimes.com/2026/01/06/us/politics/stephen-miller-foreign-policy.html#:~:text=Stephen%20Miller%20is%20a%2040%2Dyear%2Dold%20deputy%20chief,of%20constitutional%20tenets%20that%20grant%20American%20citizenship

[2] In a class I was invited to teach on the Experiential Democracy Dialogue (of all topics), I myself was "canceled" by the therapist-trainees who seemed so repelled by the idea of sitting with a person with a contrasting cultural or political view that after one class, they refused to continue the course. They also refused my subsequent offers to discuss the issue to see if we could work it out. Now I readily admit that I may have unwittingly contributed to their extreme reaction, but I never really learned how because they completely cut off communication with me. Aside from the group being purported healers, it is that latter lack of willingness to try to work the situation out that was—and is—especially concerning to me.

[3]See M. X, retold by A. Haley, *The Autobiography of Malcolm X* (One World/Penguin Random House, 1992/1965).

[4]See F. Fanon, *The Wretched of the Earth* (Grove Press, 1963) and L. Laubscher, "Frantz Fanon: Toward a new humanism." In L. Hoffman, L. Vallejos, D. Hocoy, P. Tummala-Narra, & E. DeRobertis (Eds.), *APA Handbook of Humanistic and Existential Psychology: History, Research, Philosophy, and Theory,* American Psychological Association, 2026: 219–238. https://doi.org/10.1037/0000431-009

[5]A. Camus, *The Rebel* (Vintage, 1991/1956): 300–301.

Index

E

F

G

H

Author Bio

Kirk J. Schneider, Ph.D., is a leading spokesperson for existential–humanistic psychology, an adjunct faculty member at Saybrook University and previously Teachers College, Columbia University, New York City. He is a cofounder and current president of the award-winning Existential–Humanistic Institute and was a 2022 candidate for president-elect of the American Psychological Association (APA).

Dr. Schneider is a Fellow in seven Divisions of the APA, the recipient of the Rollo May Award from Division 32 of the APA for "Outstanding and Independent Pursuit of New Frontiers in Humanistic Psychology," and author/coauthor of 16 books, along with over 200 articles and book chapters. His books include *The Paradoxical Self, Horror and the Holy, The Psychology of Existence* (with Rollo May), *Existential–Integrative Psychotherapy, The Handbook of Humanistic Psychology* (2nd edition), *Existential–Humanistic Therapy* (an APA publication now in its 3rd edition, with Orah Krug), *The Wiley World Handbook of Existential Therapy, Rediscovery of Awe, Awakening to Awe, The Spirituality of Awe, The Polarized Mind, The Depolarizing of America*, and his latest highly acclaimed book: *Life-Enhancing Anxiety: Key to a Sane World*. Several of his books have been translated into Chinese, German, Brazilian, Russian, Ukrainian, Greek, Turkish, Korean, and Lithuanian. Dr. Schneider's current focus, which draws on the psychology of Otto Rank, is on the existential bases of as well as alternatives to polarized states of being. This includes his workshops as a facilitator of the Experiential Democracy Dialogue, a one-on-one conflict mediation approach for people struggling with contrasting views and backgrounds.

Dr. Schneider's work has been featured in such outlets as the New York Times, BBC World News television, Scientific

American, CNN online, KQED's Forum program (NPR San Francisco), the Thinking Allowed PBS program with Jeffrey Mishlove, Al Jazeera's Audio platform, Vanity Fair, the Guardian, USA Today, Forbes Health, The Hill, Yahoo Life, Aeon, and Psychiatric Times. He has been a featured speaker internationally at such venues as all four World Congresses of Existential Therapy, and presented many workshops and conferences for audiences in China, Japan, Germany, France, Argentina, Lithuania, Russia, Ukraine, the UK, Italy, Greece, Korea, and Turkey, as well as nationally for the American Psychological Association, the California State Psychological Association, the New York State Psychological Association, Upstate Medical University (New York), the Global Psychology Alliance (APA), the Harvard Alumni for Mental Health, Howard University, William Alanson White Institute of Psychoanalysis (New York), and many other universities and organizations.

For more information on Dr. Schneider's work, visit https://kirkjschneider.com as well as his website offering a certificate program in the "Corps of Depth Healing" at http://corpsofdepthhealers.com. This is a free resource for depth psychological approaches to social crises, along with his YouTube channel "Corps of Depth Healers": https://www.youtube.com/@CorpsofDepthHealers-ws9nq. In addition, Dr. Schneider's podcast series with Tyler Gamlen called "Depth Dialogues" features leaders in depth psychology who apply their skills to social healing. For more information visit https://www.youtube.com/@DepthDialoguesPodcast.

Dr. Schneider is also featured in the film "The Existential Movement: Bringing Wisdom to a Turbulent World": https://www.youtube.com/watch?v=ZjVZmn28rXo as well as an upcoming film on "Bridging the Gap," a documentary investigating the political views of people across the United States on our current cultural and political divides.

www.ingramcontent.com/pod-product-compliance
Lightning Source LLC
LaVergne TN
LVHW010656110826
845149LV00014B/3116

* 9 7 8 1 9 5 5 7 3 7 7 5 3 *